MISSION AND ESCAPE DURING THE COLD WAR

The unknown story told firsthand

By

Héctor G. Aguililla

Former Cuban Diplomat Exiled in the United States

Dedication

To my late parents, Héctor M. Aguililla Diéguez and Gioconda A. Saladrigas Casañas, may they rest in peace.

To my lovely wife, Miriam Aguililla, and my dear children, Maitelis and Héctor Eduardo Aguililla.

And to my five bright grandchildren, Anastasia, Ethan, Michael, Wesley, and Lana.

Epigraph

In times of crisis, only imagination is more important than
knowledge.

Albert Einstein

Make love, not war.

John Lennon

Table of Contents

About The Author

Hector G. Aguillila was born in Havana, Cuba in 1953. He lived in Jaimanitas Beach, located in Havana, since his childhood until he fled the Cuban totalitarian regime during his trip to his last mission overseas as a Cuban government diplomat.

He married Mrs. Miriam Rodriguez Varela, also Cuban, on February 10th, 1974. That same year he graduated in

December with a Bachelor's Degree in International Relations in Havana University.

In 1976, he was appointed Third Secretary of the Cuban Foreign Service accredited in the Arab Republic of Syria. He was promoted to Second Secretary during that mission that lasted seven years until March 1984, where he also served as Second in Charge of the mission and Charge D'Affairs, a.i

Later on, during the same year, 1984, he served in a mission on a temporary basis as Second Secretary in Kuwait for four months.

From 1985 to 1987, he was assigned as Second Secretary, Second head of mission and Charge D'Affairs, a.i. in the Islamic Republic of Iran.

In 1988, he was elevated as First Secretary and Second in Charge of the Cuban embassy in the Republic of Madagascar.

During a stopover in Madrid, Spain, together with his wife and two children, he applied for political asylum in the U.S. Embassy.

On October 28th, 1988, he arrived with his family at the Andrews Air Base in Maryland, United States.

Already residing in the latter country he also studied business accounting, owned small businesses, was a realtor, loan officer, residence appraiser, car dealer, furniture salesman, and does New York stock exchange sales and purchases. He became a naturalized American citizen.

Acknowledgments

To my dear wife, Miriam Aguililla (Mirita), for having given me all her unconditional help by providing me with suggestions, data, and opinions all along.

Likewise, to my daughter Maitelis (Maite) for supporting my goals, and to my son, Héctor Eduardo (Eddy), who despite not being an editor, but an exceptionally good auditor, carried out an "audit" on my work and improved it with his sharp views and propositions.

Preface

Driven by uncommon experiences in some stages of my life while I was a Cuban diplomat, I felt motivated to write my memoirs in this narrative novel. Here, I interweave the diplomatic experience with my participation in some undercover special operations and the escape from a dictatorial regime, searching for freedom and democracy for my family's future and my own.

I took the pseudonym "Javier" when I was recruited by the Counterintelligence General Department (known as DGCI in Cuba) and the State Security General Department (known as DGSE in Cuba) for about a year, working within the diplomatic corps in Cuba before being sent to the Foreign Service for the first time in December 1976. Subsequently, I became agent "Halcon" (Falcon) for the Military Intelligence Department (known as DIM in Cuba) for several years during my mission in Syria. And in the United States, from 1988, through the CIA, I had my name legally changed to "Michael Fernandez". Seven years later, in 1995, I reverted to my birth name back as Héctor Gustavo Aguililla Saladrigas.

Eventually, after becoming a U.S. citizen, I legally kept my name as Héctor Gustavo Aguililla.

I was a Cuban Foreign Service official in countries like Syria, Iran, and Kuwait. I also served in the Ministry of Foreign Affairs (known as MINREX in Cuba)) for a total of fifteen years in the following Divisions: Legal and Consular

Affairs; International Organizations; Asia and Oceania; and Northern Africa and the Middle East.

Most of the book's narrative takes place in the Arab Republic of Syria, where I was accredited as a diplomatic agent in a mission that lasted seven years and three months; then in the Islamic Republic of Iran for a little over two years; and in the State of Kuwait for a few months.

In transit through Madrid towards my final diplomatic assignment in the Cuban embassy in Madagascar, Africa, as First Secretary and Second in Charge of the mission, I sought political asylum with my family in the U.S. Embassy in Madrid in October 1988. I was coming from Havana together with my wife, Miriam Rodríguez Varela (currently Miriam Aguililla) and my two children, Maitelis and Héctor Eduardo.

Two weeks after having escaped from the Cuban totalitarian government, we landed in the United States from Frankfurt in a military aircraft at the Andrews Air Force Base in Maryland, known as the President's Air Force Base.

In this story, I try to keep the reader focused on a narrative full of revelations of seldom-known, real events, which are usually hidden, and, sometimes, surrounded by mystique.

I depict intense years of my life during, which I really enjoyed many pleasant moments, such as cultural, diplomatic events, travels and adventures, but, on occasion, sacrifices and risks of death.

It is not easy for a person, who has been involved in notable actions and events, some of which of a historical nature, to adapt to a new regular life.

I originally wrote these memoirs with fictitious names way after more than ten years of the events having taken place, and then shelved them for another twenty years. Finally, as time went by, I decided to finish writing them with the real facts and names of people involved. Nevertheless, I left out some information and data which I did not deem prudent to reveal.

Starting with the emotional escape with my family in Madrid, Spain, followed by my beginnings as student when I was recruited by the Cuban Foreign Ministry and then my first steps as a Cuban diplomat in Syria, the narrative proceeds chronologically to maintain a clear and engaging flow.

I briefly present a general description of Syria, interesting Arab country, whose old side of its capital, Damascus, is six thousand years old, and detail my official and undercover activities, as well as visits to several cities outside the capital plus others to one neighboring country: Lebanon.

Later on, I dig into more diplomacy, intelligence and arms trafficking activities, my plans to flee Cuba, and lastly, the stay in the United States, the CIA and the FBI.

As an author, my goal is to make readers fully enjoy my memoirs and, at the same time, provide them with some international, historical, political, cultural, and religious information of interest.

I obviously include in this work the denunciation of the Cuban totalitarian dictatorship and its diabolic foreign policy of meddling and interference in various parts of the world.

CHAPTER I

ESCAPE IN MADRID

1988

We helped our daughter Maitelis to set up a farewell party she wanted to throw of her own volition at our beach house in Jaimanitas, city of Havana. She and our son Hector Eduardo (Eddy), thirteen and ten years old, respectively, had no knowledge of our secret plans to flee Cuba.

Maitelis, who was a joyful, happy, pretty and intelligent teenager, invited a group of school friends and some neighbors, but, since she was so popular, the news spread like wildfire. An impressive number of youngsters attended. The house and the porch not only got crowded, but also the attendees were dancing even in the street.

My son Eddy, also alert and intelligent, already with good aptitudes for sports, due to his young age he was an active spectator at the party.

A female neighbor, who was an informant of the State Security, reported us to the police. When the police officers arrived, I approached them, and they asked whether there was a problem. I told them I had a permit I had requested (from the police itself) for the party, and that the kids were just dancing and having fun. So, the officers said goodbye and took off.

On October 10th, 1988, a black car from the Foreign Ministry Protocol office showed up in our driveway to drive us to the airport. We made our farewells with our family members and friends who had gathered to see us off.

The female neighbor working for the State Security moved toward the car when we were ready to depart and told us:

"You are headed to a new mission of our revolution; I wish you success. You are the future of our homeland".

My wife Miriam (Mirita) with a proportionate figure, blonde, green eyes, white skin, pretty face, intelligent and a noble and friendly character, had to struggle to avoid laughing. Me too. I was a serious person of standard height, sunburnt skin, slim but with athletic body, black hair, honey-colored eyes and self-confidence.

For her part, my daughter Maitelis, also being already inside the car, spoke her mind:

"It seems to me I'm being kidnapped."

We were a little astonished, since the girl was unaware of our fleeing plans, but seemingly, a sixth sense told her something odd was going on or, maybe, it was simply an innocent comment.

At that time, due to remodeling at the International Airport in Rancho Boyeros, passengers were being checked in first somewhere else, in a place where they were bussed to the airport. The place was, by chance, located where my graduation party had been held almost fourteen years ago: Rio Cristal Park.

Another car was bringing my parents and brother-in-law, Francisco Chaviano. The latter was aware of our intentions.

At Rio Cristal, once our luggage, passports, and air tickets were checked in, we said goodbyes to our family members who accompanied us. Chaviano looked at us occasionally, with a complicit smile. We were a little nervous because we always feared that, somehow, we would be caught in the act, and, at the last minute, our departure would be halted.

We were finally taken to the Jose Marti International Airport where we took a Cubana de Aviation flight on October 10th with destination Madrid, Spain.

In the plane, Mirita and I happily smiled, aware that we still had to take the decisive step toward our goal. Flying together with us was Mr. Prieto, an official, just like me, from the Foreign Ministry, and his wife, whom we should accompany during transit in Madrid. On one hand, the idea was to serve them as guide, since this was their first flight abroad, and, on the other hand, Mr. Prieto, as a member of the Cuban Communist Party (known as PCC in Cuba)), was being used to keep an eye on us.

We arrived at Barajas International Airport in Madrid on October 11th, due to the time difference.

I tried to place our luggage in the airport checkroom while in transit to avoid them being a hindrance to our escape movement, but when I was telling the Prieto family to wait for me, I heard the voice of our director of Foreign Ministry, Ulises Estrada, who, unexpectedly called me:

"Aguililla, where are you going?"

Without showing surprise or apprehension, I cold-bloodedly answered: "Ulises, I'm going to the checkroom to drop the luggage while in transit here in Madrid to spare the taxi fare and move around with the kids easier."

"It's been a while since they last had that service in this airport", Ulises replied.

"Well, then we'll have to pay more for a taxi because they charge extra for luggage, we have no other choice", I uttered, and started to use a calculator to make estimates.

"What hotel are you going to stay in?" Ulises continued asking.

I quickly thought of telling him the truth as to where we would be lodged in case, they later checked up on us, just for the sake of not raising any suspicion "Even though we almost always stay at places such as Moderno Hotel, Monte Sol, or Arosa, this time we want to go to Coloso Hotel because it is also located relatively near Puerta del Sol and the big department stores like Galerias Preciados and El Corte Ingles", replied.

"Yeah", Ulises asserted, "I know it. I've stayed there. It's a good place. Take Prieto and his wife with you".

"Don't worry. They are in good hands; I didn't know you were on the same flight". I said and asked him, what are you doing around here?

I had realized Ulises had flown first class and had boarded the plane in Havana through the protocol section without either being noticed or saying a word to us. No wonder he was called "The Black Panther" by some officers in the CIA. Ulises, a tall person with shaved head and black skin, had been second head of the Department of America from the intelligence, then commanded by Manuel Piñeiro, former Deputy Interior Ministry, known as "Commander Barbaroja" (red beard), in charge of the Cuban penetration and subversion, mainly in Latin America.

"I'm headed to Algiers to take part in a meeting of the Economic Cooperation Joint Committee between Algeria and Cuba" Ulises answered me.

"Good luck. I'm sure you're going to be fine" I concluded.

Right afterwards, we headed out to take the taxi with the luggage. I got Mr. Prieto and his wife in a cab first, telling the driver their destination and to follow our car so Mr. Prieto would not suspect anything at all. Mirita, the kids, and I took another cab.

On the way to the hotel, while talking with the driver, we realized the next day would be October 12th, a national holiday in Spain celebrating the discovery of the Americas and the advent of the Spanish Empire.

I guessed the U.S. Embassy would be closed. In general, diplomatic missions respect holidays of the host country.

On seeing I would not be able to conduct my plans the next day after our arrival, as initially conceived, my brain started to work a million revolutions per second. It occurred to me that maybe I could bribe the taxi driver by offering him a one-hundred-dollar bill in order for him to run away from the other taxi following us and go straight to the U.S. Embassy. After I surreptitiously showed Mirita the bill and made a signal about my intentions, she answered with a negative gesture disapproving of my idea. Since the kids were traveling with us, I ruled it out.

We arrived at the hotel at about 1 pm and booked three rooms on the second floor. By chance, Mr. Prieto and his wife's room was across from the elevator and stairs and ours at the end of the hallway.

"Prieto" I told him, "The best we can do now is go to bed and rest for a few hours due to the long trip (ten-hour flight) and by four, we can go shopping. Here in Madrid, most stores close at noon and open again from four to nine"

"Agreed" Mr. Prieto said," we are also sleepy, and we aren't hungry, because of what we ate during the flight".

Once in the room, I told Mirita to check that the carry-on bags with which we planned, to escape carried the essentials because I was going to make a call out of the hotel.

I had to walk several blocks to find a public phone booth. All were busy but I waited and got one available. I was a little worried because close to me, there was a man who was frequently touching the back of one ear where I could see a bulge, which made me think it could be a listening device, but I calmed down right away. If someone was being watched, it was not me, since it was impossible for them to have someone planted there to keep watching over me, because I had gone there unexpectedly.

Once I managed to get through with the U.S. Embassy in Madrid, the conversation was as follows:

"U.S. Embassy. Good afternoon: How may we help you?"

"Please, could I speak with His Excellency, the ambassador, Mr. Reginald Bartholomew?" I spoke.

"Sir, may I know who's calling him?" the operator replied.

"Yes, tell him this is a Latin American diplomat friend of his in transit through Madrid" I replied.

"Well, I'm gonna transfer you to the ambassador's personal Secretary, bear with me, please".

"I'm sorry, but the ambassador is not in right now. If you wish, you can leave him a message. I'm his personal secretary. Could you tell me your name?" his secretary finally asked.

"My name is Hector Aguililla Saladrigas, First Secretary of the Republic of Cuba, I'm in transit here in Madrid headed to Madagascar, but I want to apply for political asylum in your embassy with my wife and children".

"Bear with me, Mr. Hector, I'm going to turn to the person in charge of these affairs" said the secretary, who quickly asked: "How long would it take you to get to the embassy?"

"I need you to send two cars to the hotel" I specified, "one that allows us to leave the hotel and another to stay and pick up our luggage".

"Hector, I'm sorry, but the person in charge of these affairs is not in the embassy now, as I said. Could you take a taxi?" he asked me.

"Yes, of course, we can take a taxi" I responded.

"How long will it take you to reach the embassy" he asked me.

"I guess we'll be there in about forty-five minutes. Remember, I'll be going with my wife and children. Whom should I call when I arrive?"

"Ask for Pedro. I'll be waiting for you by the gate."

I hung up and felt relieved, since to me, that conversation was the key step towards a leap to freedom. I looked around, and there still was the guy who, suspiciously, pressed the back of his ear, but I did not see anything out of the ordinary and returned to the Coloso Hotel, where Mirita was waiting anxiously.

When I got back to the hotel, I told the front desk employee that "we would be away for a couple of days because we'd be visiting friends away from Madrid and would leave the luggage in the room, and, please, do not hand them to anyone, not even members of my embassy themselves if they showed up because we would be back"- I added. "And please, call a taxi because we are leaving in ten minutes."

Mirita was already waiting with the carry-on bags. We woke up the kids, who were innocently sleeping in the other room without knowing their future and destiny would change from that moment on. We just told them we would be visiting some friends; then Maitelis asked whether she could pick up something, she had put away in the night table when we arrived. Of course, we did not object: they were bangles and fancy jewelry she loved.

We went down the hallway cautiously and silently and keeping an eye on the door to the room where Mr. Prieto and his wife were pleasantly sleeping.

We took the elevator and down by the lobby, I asked about the taxi, but I was told it had already gone.

I reiterated to the employee that we were leaving luggage in our room, which they should not be given to anyone, and that we would be back in a few days.

I picked up our passports we had left at the front desk, as it was usual in Madrid, and we went out looking for a taxi.

I looked overhead and saw the Pietro family's room window, where my "vigilante" was sleeping without a trace of suspicion. I decided to walk, and a few steps later, we waived for a taxi. Once inside, I told the driver:

"Take us to the U.S. Embassy, but please hurry up because I have an important interview there".

The driver happened to be an old man, who, after fixing his beret on his head and looking carefully through the side view mirrors, slowly started to drive the old car.

"Sir" I told him, "It's getting late, hurry, please, I'm gone to miss my interview".

"This is not how it works, calm down, I can't rush, we're moving. We're moving", the old man protested.

The cab driver kept driving at his pace, but it seemed that the displeasure in my face made him go faster as he looked at me through the rearview mirror.

We finally made it to the U.S. Embassy. I felt as if it had been the longest trip of my life. When we got out of the car, I handed the driver a two-thousand Spanish peseta bill, and without waiting for the change, I told Mirita to follow me with the kids.

I opened the gate of the U.S. diplomatic mission leading to the consular section and found a line of people and two guards in front of them.

While walking in, I looked at the big front door of the building with a staircase ahead and saw no one waiting for me.

I showed the guards our passports and in a loud voice so all the ones in the line would hear me, I said:

"Diplomats, diplomats", showing our passports with a raised hand.

A few moments later, two or three people came out through the main door of the building, and I also asked them with a loud voice:

"Pedro? Pedro?"

And someone answered:

"Let them go through, let them in".

Already inside, our carry-on bags went through a metal detector device. The U.S. diplomat allegedly called Pedro (maybe it was Peter) showed us into an office.

The kids were strained and did not utter a word, because they realized something strange, and grave was brewing. They were very smart, respected us and trusted their parents.

In October 1988, we were in the later years of the cold war (1945-1991), before the fall of the Berlin Wall in November 1989, and before the disintegration of the Soviet Union in November 1991, which marked the end of that period.

Once in the office of a U.S official, who identified himself as Mike, and who happened to be the head of the CIA in Madrid, I explained to him:

"We wish to apply for political asylum because we are escaping from the Cuban communist system, and we want to live in freedom and democracy in order to have a better future for our children and ourselves, I guess", I kept saying," you must know that recently the CIA failed an operation carried out by the former Cuban official and defector Florentino Azpillaga, when he tried to recruit a First Secretary of the Cuban Embassy in London. Such First Secretary refused to defect and violently attacked Azpillaga, who ended up hurt. That Cuban official was welcomed as a hero when he returned to Havana by Fidel Castro, who awarded him with a medal of honor."

"The Cuban intelligence took this occasion to announce its alleged successes in their fight against the CIA. It disclosed on TV and a publication that about twenty double spies infiltrated the CIA. Besides, they aired videos of intelligence operations by CIA agents, who were members of the U.S. Interest Section in Havana, aimed at trying to discredit the CIA and showing purported triumphs of the revolution to the population. As you are supposed to know, I kept saying, they will be very happy in Virginia and Washington once they find out about my defection, precisely at a juncture in which the balance was not on your side."

"I perfectly understand" Mike said. "Would you like to drink or eat something, or use the restrooms?", he asked.

"Yes, we'd like to go to the restrooms", I answered.

Mike, a tall person, of about forty-five years old with brown hair, called an aide who guided us to the restrooms.

When we left the office, I observed all the doors had combination locks and there were cameras on the ceiling.

We came out of the restrooms, and Eddy approached me and told me in a low tone:

"Daddy, I memorized the door lock combination numbers. You must push numbers xx...".

"Great, Eddy", I told him while winking at him as a sign of complicity. "Don't forget them. But don't worry, everything is gonna be fine."

I was really impressed by the gumption and cunning of my son, who was just ten years old, but I realized the tense and uncertain mindset showing in both of my kids' faces. The above was a product of a constant ideological brainwashing in Cuba, where they were instilled that the Americans were the bad guys and our enemies.

Then I asked Mike:

"Would you give us a few minutes to speak with the kids alone?"

"Yeah" he replied, "then I'll make some arrangements".

In a very simple way, Mirita and I explained to our children, what was going on and the reasons for that. That relaxed them a bit.

After we finished our conversation with the kids, Mike came back and asked us:

"Would you rather stay in a hotel nearby or in the outskirts of Madrid?"

"In none of the two", I reacted, "I'd rather stay here in this office to stay the night, don't worry about us".

I knew when Mr. Prieto found out, we had vanished, he would call the Cuban Embassy and its staff would try to track us and get us back.

"OK. I got another choice", Mike added, "we can take you to a safe place in one our air force base outside Madrid. How about that?"

"Perfect", I immediately shot back, but I'd like you to know I'm not going to split from my family ever.

"Ok. I understand. We'll leave in three cars to the base, and you will all be in one of them", Mike specified.

A few minutes later, we left. The three cars were waiting by the embassy's main gate for us with drivers and bodyguards. The drive lasted about forty minutes.

We headed to the air base in Torrejon de Ardoz, twenty-two kms. from Madrid. The base was operated by both Spain and the United States until 1992, when the United States stopped its operations as a result of the end of the cold war.

14

I logically knew the CIA would be interested in the information, I could have and that was why we were treated well.

When we arrived at the base, we were lodged in a large suite, which I guess, was for high-level visitors. The suite was big and cozy. It had a big double-bed bedroom, a dining/living room, and a bar. We then started to cool down.

We were offered coffee, and Mirita accepted it due to a headache she had, but she did not drink it because it was an American-style, too watered-down coffee for our habits, and did not like it.

Mike warned us to be careful, when speaking near the Spanish maids. Evidently, the Spanish government was not informed of the operation, at least, until we left the country.

After we were accommodated, Mike and a base intelligence officer knocked on the door. We sat by the bar and had a drink. Mike started speaking and in a very natural way said:

"I was asked that you gave us, some examples of your experience or knowledge of matters of interest for us, and we're going to report it right away. It's very important, since our interest in you depends on that a lot."

I figured out they wanted to assess the importance of the Information I could have, and the treatment and available resources for us could depend on that. Besides, I guessed, without a doubt, the request came down from the CIA general headquarters in Langley, Virginia.

"Ok, Mike, but let your superiors know that I'm not coming with the intent of either selling or negotiating anything. I'll provide the collaboration I deem convenient to fight Castro's dictatorship and international terrorism. We just need help to get to the United States and have a chance to start a new life in liberty and democracy. You may take down the following points", I told him.

1- Secret trip to Cuba by an alleged defecting CIA officer, accompanied by a Cuban DGI officer, from Damascus.

2- Undercover operations of shipment of weapons and ammo, made by the West countries and Israel, from Syria to Cuba bound to narcoguerrilla organizations in Latin America.

3- Secret directives from the Cuban Foreign Ministry Department 1, created by the Armed Forces Military Intelligence Division, to coordinate plans for defense and resistance abroad during the so-called "Special Period".

4- Knowledge about some terrorists in Syria and Lebanon.

5- Contradictions and inner problems within the Cuban government, especially in the Foreign Ministry and its Foreign Service.

6- Cuban foreign policy and its bilateral relations with Iraq, Iran, Syria, the Palestinian organizations, and the Middle East in general.

"Mike", I added, "stress in your report that I'll provide information and possibly more, when I am settled with my family in the United States".

"I believe they have enough material to work with you for at least eight months", Mike commented.

"Yes, now everything depends on the fact that my family and I are given a fast and safe arrival in the United States."

"I'm sure you'll be welcomed", Mike asserted, "You're going to enjoy freedom and democracy with your family, since unfortunately, you don't have them in your country. You'll see that everything there is progress, always going up".

For communists back in Cuba, I would be a "traitor", but for the people well informed on the Cuban reality, it was obvious that the only real traitor in Cuba was the psychopath President Fidel Castro and his clique. He not only committed treason and betrayed the entire population, but also to the international community, when he established socialism in transit to communism in Cuba and led the country to the most degrading misery in a dictatorial totalitarian system, lack of individual freedom, human rights, expression and information.

By defecting from that system, I was hitting the tyrant with a big blow. For different circumstances or reasons, many had been able to flee the country, but others remained within fighting the regime by diverse means.

That night, we could rest and sleep peacefully despite the situation we were in.

The next morning, we boarded a small six-seat jet plane that was waiting for us very close from where we were staying in the base.

We were politely seen off by the base commander dressed in an elegant, white gala uniform.

We headed to Frankfurt and enjoyed the private flight. Even the kids had fun, because one of the pilots allowed them to handle a small control in the aircraft that made the small plane tilt or turn left of right while on autopilot.

We arrived at the U.S. Rhein-Main Air Force Base located next to the Frankfurt International Airport:

There at the airbase we contacted Richard, a CIA officer. We departed from Frankfurt air force base to another U.S. Air Force base in Ramstein in a small convoy made up of three Mercedes Benz cars. Richard, who was the CIA head at the Ramstein base, traveled in the first car; on the second one, traveling were my wife, our two children, and I; and the last one was occupied by Mike, the CIA center head in Madrid, plus a military intelligence official from the air force base in the outskirts of Madrid, of Cuban origin, who came to accompany us throughout our stay in Europe.

We made a couple of stops on our way to eat and drink something. Before long we could watch the development with which, with a naked eye, could be seen in Germany. In the past, we had only been able to get to know the Berlin side of the Democratic (communist) Germany.

"I'm impressed by the cleanliness, the pattern of farmlands and their houses, the quality of life and the high technological level that could be seen right away" I said, "Is there the same living standard in the United States as here?" I asked Richard during one of the stops to rest.

"You asked an interesting question", Richard replied. "The standard of living of the average German citizen in this country is higher than that of a U.S. citizen at present. That carries its political reasons, but we can't leave out the inherent merits of the German people who are well-organized and talented. These traits are largely the result of the ideological, cold war between the two big systems: the capitalist one and the communist one".

"This is the Federal Republic of Germany", Richard continued, "a mirror of the capitalist system achievements in Europe, and opposing it is the so-called German Democratic

Republic, a mirror of the communist alleged accomplishments. That's why Russia always has a steady intravenous drip" aid on communist Germany, while we do the same with our ally".

When we arrived at the Ramstein U.S. base we were introduced to another CIA officer, whose pseudonym was David, and who traveled from Virginia specifically to care for and escort us on our journey to Washington". David would be our "Babysitter". He is a tall and strong person, with white skin, friendly, intelligent and good person.

Ramstein US Air Force Base (about 80 miles from Frankfurt), located in Rhineland-Palatinate, a state in southwestern Germany, serves as the headquarters for the United States Air Forces in Europe and NATO Allied Air Command:

At Ramstein Airbase, we had medical checkups done. Also, and a psychologist specialist came from Washington to do some screening on us.

I also signed a proxy authorizing the U.S. Embassy in Madrid, to pick our luggage up at the Coloso Hotel by describing them and its approximate weight.

Mike told us, they had found out the Cuban Embassy had tried to take away such luggage, but the hotel staff refused to let them do it due to the request I made before leaving of not handing it to anybody. Also, there was a bunch of about ten Cuban agents looking for us all over Madrid. For a few days, they were befuddled without confirmation of my defection.

In order to send a message to our family members in Cuba, I had agreed, before leaving Cuba, to send a telegram to my brother-in-law, Francisco Chaviano, once things had gone as planned. The telegram code was: "We are fine. I already bought you what you needed". This message would mean that everything had gone plain sailing, and he could give my parents a hidden letter for them. Such a telegram was sent by Mike through an Asian country so Cuba would be clueless as to our whereabouts.

Chaviano was later jailed because of his trying to leave Cuba illegally and, due to his antigovernment activities, was sentenced to fifteen years in prison as a political prisoner falsely charged with disclosing state secrets to the enemy.

After serving his sentence as a political prisoner of conscience, he continued his battle in Cuba, founded the National Council for Civil Rights, and became one of the main leaders of the Cuban Democratic Alliance. In 2012, he emigrated together with my sister, Ana Aguililla, as a former political prisoner asylee. From that point on, he continued his opposition to the regime through journalistic means and by joining organizations of former political prisoners in exile.

When the authorization for our entry into the United States finally arrived in Ramstein after being there for fifteen days, we returned to the Frankfurt base the same way we had come.

That US air force base Rhein-Main, then located next to the Frankfurt International Airport, was closed down in 2005, and its area was used to expand the airport.

We were lodged in a hotel within the US Frankfurt air force base. When we were going to enter the elevator, Mirita and the kids got in first. Someone put the luggage in, and the only room left inside was taken by agent David. On realizing I would be left out, I, without hesitation and quickly, took out two bags, left them in the lobby, and went into the elevator. Everybody stared at each other silently. Later, our bags were taken upstairs by a soldier with Asian traits and a peculiar, contagious smile which made us all laugh, especially the kids.

The next day, we flew in a U.S. cargo plane, a DC 10, which served as an ambulance carrying some injured personnel. We were accompanied by David, the CIA official.

During the flight, surgery was performed in a stretcher near our seats. The kids threw up despite having taken pills to avoid vomiting. We arrived about twelve hours later at our final destination.

We entered the United States through the Andrews Air Force Base in Maryland used by the country's presidents:

We were greeted at the runway by an escort with a van and another car. We left the base and were driven a long ride to avoid being followed, which made my son Eddy, and my wife Mirita get dizzy. Finally, we were taken to a house located near the base.

CHAPTER II

BEGINNINGS

1969

I was summoned for an interview at the Marianao High School 'Manolito Aguiar' in Havana, where I was studying my next-to-last grade year. I did not know what it was about, just that it was to be done by "Government People".

I was a young man with just sixteen years old and many dreams and expectations for my future.

I was born in Marianao, Havana, but I grew up since I was three in Jaimanitas Beach, a coastal town west of Havana, next to the current "Marina Hemingway" (formerly known as Barlovento) and separated from the latter by the Jaimanitas River bridge. Also close by is Santa Fe Beach, on the marina's other side.

Jaimanitas is a town with a population mainly made up of fishermen, workers, and a middle-class minority. My house was built with blocks and concrete, owned by my late parents.

The town lies by the banks and mouth of Jaimanitas River, from which the town took its name, and had a quarry of limestone, widely used in construction, called "Jaimanitas Stones" since 1943.

The river mouth, a fishing center, and the beach played an important role in recreational and economic activities, especially in the summertime. Many bars and clubs sprang into existence and later, bigger seaside resorts were built such as "El Cabo Parrado" (Los Marinos), "La Conchita", "La Sociedad", and "Lucilo de la Peña", called "Marcelo Salado" nowadays. The latter has been allotted to the service of sectors of the so-called Light Industry during Castros' government. The same happens with the river inlet, currently taken up by the Border Guard Troops.

Jaimanitas River:

Map of Jaimanitas location in Havana Cuba:

View of city of Havana from the coast of Jaimanitas beach:

There is also an area in Jaimanitas that became the residential area of Fidel Castro, his wife, Dalia Soto del Valle, and family, which is called "Point Zero". The Jaimanitas Stone quarry once was around that area, and there was a golf course in another area nearby. The latter was estimated to be a seventy-acre field.

*Map of **Punto Zero**, Former Bunker of Fidel Castro in Jaimanitas:*

The town residents had no access to that area; they simply had to go along its edge. It is well guarded by members of personal security and its surveillance cameras. Within the area, there are several houses, a helicopter pad, horse barns, a self-sufficient farm (lamb, fowl, and other animals), a swimming pool, a library, and a military base.

Point Zero is on one side of Fifth Avenue, and on the other side, right across, are the yacht piers with access to the sea in an area where the Interior Ministry Special Troops command was posted.

Years later, that place on the coast facing Point Zero was led by the Army Forces Counterintelligence Central Command.

During my youth, I played almost all popular sports played in a tropical country, with horse riding, swimming, skin diving, and hunting being my favorite ones.

My parents had middle-class status. My lovely mother, Gioconda A. Saladrigas Casañas, R.I.P., was a tenured professor and a Catholic. Her father, Gustavo Adolfo Saladrigas, was an architect, and her mother, Ana Casañas, a music teacher. A cousin of her father's, Carlos Saladrigas y Zayas, was a lawyer, politician, and diplomat. He held offices of Foreign Minister (1933), senator (1936-40), Minister of Justice (1934), Ambassador to the United Kingdom (1935), Prime Minister (1940-1942), and Minister of War, Navy, and National Defense (1942).

In 1944, Carlos Saladrigas ran as a candidate for the Democratic Socialist Coalition, but elections were won by Ramon Grau San Martin, a candidate for the Republican Authentic Alliance. The former returned as State Minister from 1955 to 1956, during General Batista's government's third term.

My late father, Hector Manuel Aguililla Dieguez, was from Jiguani, a city in the former province of Oriente, Cuba. His parents, Ramon Eduardo (Lalo) Aguililla Gongora, and Brigida Dieguez, had a farm with several "caballerias" (1 caballeria equaled 33.16 acres of land).

During his youth, my father moved to Havana to study and graduated as an industrial electrician technician. He took up training in the U.S. city of Atlanta on aircraft electricity and worked for the Havana International Airport as well as for a U.S. company called Bristol. He was a professor of electricity in a technological institute and, besides, was a head of a department in charge of the electricity, automation, and control of the Sugar Ministry, and head of the instrumentation workshop of Toledo Sugar Mill in the city of Havana.

Politically speaking, my father always fought for the workers' rights and claims. He was the union general secretary of the Sugar Ministry, but never a member of the Communist Party.

I have two sisters, the older one being Isis Brigida Aguililla Saladrigas, a meteorologist. She took ballet and piano courses. She was an excellent student and was always set as an example to be followed in school. The younger one, Ana Belgica Aguililla Saladrigas, graduated with a bachelor's degree in English teaching. She has always been a strong opponent of the Castro's totalitarian regime in Cuba, as director of a digital magazine and, together with her husband, Francisco Chaviano, ex-political prisoner of conscience, dissident leader, and a journalist in exile.

When the Castros' dictatorship took over in Cuba in 1959 and opened the path to socialism and communism, I was only five years old. All the schools became public under government control so the regime could ideologically indoctrinate children and young people.

My last two years in middle school (up to ninth grade), were in Liberty City School: a group of buildings where the formerly known Columbia Military Barracks of ex-president Fulgencio Batista were.

I graduated from high school at 17 in the Marianao Institute "Manolito Aguiar".

I arrived at the institute classroom, where I had been summoned for an interview. I felt well, comfortable, relaxed, with the confidence and energy youth brings. It was the first official or work interview in my lifetime and I did not have the slightest idea of what proper clothes to wear or procedure of rules to follow or the behavior I should have.

A tall man asked me to sit down. Without much preamble, he explained to me that he was an official from the Foreign Ministry's Cadre and Personnel Division, and that I was among the twenty-one short-listed students from my school to be interviewed. That among those twenty-one pre-selected ones only three finalists would be chosen to study in the Foreign Service Institute, affiliated at that time only to the Foreign Ministry (it was a few years later integrated to Havana University).

The Foreign Ministry official asked me personal, educational, economic, and political routine questions like, for example, if I believed the upcoming 1970 ten-million-ton sugar harvest, to which Commander-in-Chief Fidel had committed himself to, would be accomplished.

My father, who was the head of a department in the Sugar Industry Ministry, had told me that its minister had been removed from his post because he had expressed his opinion stating that the ten-million-ton harvest could not be achieved. He would never hold a top position again. On my mind, I had to say what the interviewer would allegedly like to hear, so, without thinking twice, I answered I was sure that the ten million would be fulfilled thanks to the people's participation and backing.

At that moment, anyone who did not say that he or she endorsed that fantasy, dreamed of only by Fidel's delusional mind, was considered as ideologically weak, an individual who did not trust the "Revolution", and even regarded as a counterrevolutionary. That obviously meant to have no future within the system in which I started to evolve with "Double Morals". I filled out all the required forms and applications, since it looked like a great choice to study international relations, above all, because of the chances to travel abroad to get to know the real world, to be able to make progress, and escape from that stagnated society, which, instead of the country moving forward, it was already evident it was experiencing a regression in all fields.

About three months later, the high school principal told me I had been picked, together with another two students,

Nestor Sosa, and Rodolfo Blain, to study at the international relations school once we graduated from high school. To this end, we would receive a notice from the Foreign Ministry once we got the high school degree.

I did not really expect that news, because I had had a personal mishap with the school principal himself, whose last name was Arambarri, when we almost had a fight. That happened because he took away a book belonging to my father that I was improperly reading in class. In a bullying attitude, abusing his authority, and with a lack of respect, he dared me to get the book from his desk, by saying "if you are a man", which I did, which caused other teachers present to intercede. This Mr. Arambarri was originally a physical education teacher but despite that, in my opinion, was not fit to be a principal, but he had been appointed for political reasons, since he was a trusted member of the communist party (known as PCC in Cuba).

After I finished the final exams in the High School, I enjoyed my vacation without having received any news from the Foreign Ministry. So, I had enrolled in mechanical engineering in the university, because I really liked sciences more than arts. However, when I least expected it, I received a plain telegram at home, which stated I was being summoned for an interview in the Foreign Ministry located in Vedado, Havana. When I showed up, I was informed that my selection and background check had been concluded, and I would begin taking classes at the Foreign Service Institute in early January 1971. Also, I went through several psychological tests, the results of which were kept in secrecy. Later, I could find out, through unofficial sources, that the results had been excellent.

I began my new studies in makeshift rooms in the Foreign Ministry itself. Three months later, the first cut of some students started. They were expelled because they were criticized for their alleged "Extravagant Clothing", "Ideological Diversionim", and even "homosexuality".

A building intended for the Foreign Service Institute was finally remodeled in Miramar, Havana, where we carried on with our classes.

We students were originally from various places and institutes from all over the country: high schools, members of the Communist Party selected from the Party's National School, Ñico Lopez; the Revolutionary Armed Forces Ministry; the Interior Ministry; and officials from the Foreign Ministry itself, who were expected to excel and improve themselves. Also, children of high-ranking officials and martyrs of the revolution were included. After four grade years, only about seventy percent of us graduated.

The deputy minister at the time, Captain Carlos Chain, told us we were going to be "a new revolutionary infusion of new blood in the ministry in order to do away with the old bourgeous traits and bad habits inherited from capitalism".

We passed several educational, psychological, ideological, and political screenings during our training. The objective logically was, above all, to be extensively indoctrinated into the marxist-leninist ideology and political economics. Then came learning languages, history (part of it a version from the points of view of the dictatorship), philosophy, international law, consular affairs, literature, grammar, diplomatic protocol standards, and culture in general.

Students who flunked a subject were automatically excluded from the institute. Likewise, those who were severely criticized in quarterly assessment meetings; those who wore "Extravagant" clothes; the ones who did not take part in "Voluntary" work in agriculture or construction; the absentees to night watch in their neighborhood's Committees for the Defense of the Revolution and the institute itself; and, above all, those considered ideologically immature, that is, the ones who did not uncompromisingly defend the alleged "Principles" of the socialist revolution.

We were educated by the best teachers the country had at the time, such as historians Manuel Moreno Fraginal, professor Orlando Dubuche; international law specialists Dr. Miguel D'Estefano and Dr. Olga Miranda Bravo; the Foreign Minister himself, Dr. Raul Roa Garcia and his son, Raul Roa Kouri, too; and other renown personalities. Among the latter were Aleida March, Ernesto "Che" Guevara's widow; Carlos

Perez, a graduate of Marxism-Leninism high studies in the Soviet Union, former professor of the Party's National School, Ñico Lopez, and ex-economic adviser of vice-president Raul Castro; and ambassadors and experienced directors from the Foreign Ministry. Other ministers such as Ricaro Cabrisas from the Foreign Trade Ministry, and several distinguished personalities gave us lectures.

One of my classmates, Valentin Dominguez, married the above-mentioned professor, Aleida March, Che Guevara's widow. He personally told me that she had to ask Fidel for permission to marry again.

On one occasion, I went with Valentin to study at what once had been Ernest Che Guevara's personal office, where you could find documents made by Che Guevara on some African and Latin American countries, the likes of which he used to try to export the revolution by means of guerrilla warfare.

Classmates in the Higher Institute of International Relations (known as ISRI in Cuba) were a son of Ramon (Mongo) Castro, a Fidel's brother; the son of Jesus (Chucho) Montane Oropesa, member of the PCC's Politburo; two children of Major Tony Santiago Garcia, martyr of G2 and State Security; the son of Raul Valdes Vivo, also member of the PCC's Central Committee; and other children of the governing elite. Of the above-privileged ones, only the son of Jesus Montane and the two children of late Tony Santiago graduated. To be precise, the son of Jesus Montane, Sergio, graduated a year after I did.

The General Secretary of the institute's party called me a year and a half before our graduation to tell me that he advised me to break up with my girlfriend Miriam, because she had been issued a passport to leave the country, and that would be harmful for me in a future consideration for a Foreign Service position. I appreciated his suggestions and told him I would seriously give it a thought. Mirita and I already had plans to get married in the near future and the passport he alluded to had been issued when she was a minor several years ago. Then, what she did was to quickly become a member of the Young Communist League aimed at offsetting such a comment on the passport. Never again did I hear about it.

I took martial arts classes offered by a former member of the Cuban Interior Ministry's Special Forces, which originated from an old school of Korean origin called Kuk Sool Won; the latter comprises all the other martial arts facets. It was the first technique used by the Cuban Foreign Ministry's Special Troops when they were first set up, and as we were told, it means "the fastest way to kill".

Kuk Sool Won combines kicking, hand strikes, projections, trips, armlocks, falls, fall brakings, joint locking, pressure points, body conditioning as well as mental development, and training with traditional weapons within a strong and, at the same time, soft style, based on speed and flow.

My military training was brief, but in a militaristic regime, almost everybody had taken some of it. Still as a child, I became a member of the so-called Revolutionary Youth Patrols, where we would march wearing yellow shirts and wooden shotgun replicas.

The first firearm I used was a compressed air "pellet shotgun". I had a good markmanship and went bird hunting frequently. Once, unknowingly, I killed a very pretty little bird called "bee hummingbird" or "Colibri" in Cuba, which is very small and is in motion all the time. It is a small bird, the hunting of which is prohibited because it is an endangered species. That is why I was reprimanded by my uncle Cuco, a hunter, but at the same time he was impressed by my hunting it with an ordinary pellet shotgun, because the bee hummingbird is almost always in constant motion. Also, with the same shotgun, I hit a quail standing in a nearby bush in the head from a Jeep, which also amazed my uncle, an expert hunter.

Not long after, still as a child, I used an automatic. "22 Caliber Shotgun" with a telescope sight. The holes it opened in white-tailed mourning doves, whistling ducks, and other birds were awfully big, but we would freeze them and later cook them.

Later on, in high school militia training, I used an old rifle called "Mauser", which we were given with three bullets to do guard duty without proper training.

In the Foreign Ministry, as the head of a militia company, for the first time I used a Walther PPK handgun.

Parallel to the militia in the Foreign Ministry, I was a member of the so-called Territorial Troops Militias (known as MTT in Cuba). There I was trained to shoot with a Russian anti-aircraft four-barrel machine gun.

I remember, once we carried out a real-life drill against a very small plane pulled by another plane in real flight. That day, the platoon lieutenant in charge of men and women, assigned a young woman in my squad to shoot that weapon. She seemingly volunteered and he, to please her, agreed, but she was not trained enough and, therefore, was not ready for that task; she possibly had not taken a shot with anything at all. I disagreed with the lieutenant's decision, but he did not change his mind. Later I found out, that they were relatives.

After giving the coordinates, I gave the order to shoot our atillery weapon because at the time we only had a chance for one shot. I repeated the order three times and the target went beyond our reach without a single shot made. A captain came to me right away to criticize me because I had had to push the pedal with the hands myself to shoot if the young woman failed to follow orders and did not use her foot.

The captain was right but, the real blame fell on the lieutenant for not listening to me and placing the unprepared and inexperienced young girl in that position.

After that, I never returned to the militia practice, despite it was something that gave me credit, but I realized that militias were somehow militarily ineffective, and rather had a political calling in order to keep the people's minds busy thinking of alleged imminent invaders. If the regime counted on these militias to really take on an eventual American attack, they were lost.

One day, while at home, I received a telegram from the military committee's office summoning me to show up two days later at 6 a.m. at the Dog Race Track in Marianao Beach, and instructing me to bring a toothbrush and toothpaste (a typical message for a call to mandatory military service). I showed the telegram to the Foreign Ministry director of Cadres and Personnel, who got from the then Deputy Minister, Capitan Chaun, a signed letter for me to take personally to the military office. I was released from military service, classified in the category of "indispensable for the country's economy", another incongruity of the system, written on my ID.

I learned French very well; I acquired mid-level in English, and I brought my mother tongue, Spanish, to perfection. I obtained excellent grades and passed all the periodic screenings of political and educational purges during the four-year career.

I finally graduated in 1974, and a ceremony was held at the Havana National Theater, where I was awarded a diploma. Due to bureaucratic red tape with Havana University, the title of Bachelor's in International Relations was given to us later. We were regarded as "the new man" or "the creme d'la crème" of the new generation formed by the revolution.

A great celebration was arranged at Rio Cristal Park, where champagne bottles were placed on all tables for the guests, and a nice buffet was available. Besides, one of the best popular orchestras at the time played all along.

Accompanying me was Mirita, who was expecting our future daughter Maitelis. We had gotten married ten months before at the Havana Marriage Palace, and had thrown a rather quiet party at my place. We spent a one-week honeymoon at the Riviera Hotel, which was our favorite one. We also went to Varadero Beach for a week.

In Varadero, Mirita had two accidents. The first one was at the Oasis Hotel swimming pool. I knew she could not swim very well, but young at heart, as a prank, I pushed her into the pool and saw her sink with her arms reaching up until the water gobbled her up. I realized she was really drowning. Thank God, I was physically fit and swimming and skin diving were my forte, so I hastily dove into the pool, grabbed her at the pool bottom and pulled her up little by little until we saw the light and reached the surface. I did not know what to do or say to apologize, but she, always so adorable, understood what happened and did not complain about it.

Another day, we rented a couple of horses for a ride away from the hotel. Mirita's horse sat on the ground, so she called for help. Hence, I got close to her but, inexplicably, the horse got up and started to run wild at full speed. I followed her but I could not catch up with her and saw the horse was headed to a heavily trafficked highway. I yelled telling her to pull the reins back to stop and detour the horse, but the horse did not take orders. Then I saw a truck coming down the road while her horse was nearing the latter and eventually crossed it. Seconds later, the truck went by and, if not for a few seconds difference, it would have caused a tragic accident. I ultimately crossed the road on horseback, too, until I could finally reach her and help her to stop the horse. Since we were young, almost everything was obviously an adventure and fun.

As Mirita lived in the city of Placetas for many years and still had close relatives living there, we would visit almost every year. We would have a good time because we would go to the city's cabaret, got together with friends, threw parties, and traveled to other nearby cities like Santa Clara and Caibarien.

Additionally, we took the opportunity to go to the countryside and get agricultural provisions to take back to Havana due to the food scarcity in the city. One I liked most was a very good homemade, creamy, white cheese made by the area's farmers, and black beans, too.

Mirita had an uncle who was the administrator of a place with a big freezer. There we stored pigs, goats, a turkey, and chicken I hunted and skinned so we would freeze them and later put in the car trunk to go back to Havana.

During my last grade year, I had worked part-time as a specialist assistant in the Asia and Oceania Division and the International Organization Division, where I had on-the-job training.

I started to work full-time in 1975 as a specialist on Syria, Lebanon, and Jordan in the Foreign Ministry's Division of North Africa and the Middle East.

In March of that year, 1975, my daughter Maitelis was born, which encouraged us to keep thriving.

Due to the ceremony of the Cuban Communist Party's First Congress in December 1975, the Central Committee's International Relations Department instructed us to hold conferences on the countries of delegations invited to different centers in the country.

Together with another official of my department, we teamed up to hold conferences on the Palestinian Resistance and Lebanon to workers from a Matanzas province sugar mill and students from Havana University in their amphitheater where questions were asked at the end.

I continued to take one-hour English classes a day in the afternoons at the Ministry's Training Department. And at night, I would take the associate classes of the Bachelor's in History as a second major in Havana University, but I could not finish the latter because I was assigned to work for the Foreign Service.

I had several directors, among them, personalities such as Ulises Estrada Lescaille, who clandestinely fought against Fulgencio Batista's dictaratorship as a member of the July 26 Movement, and later became an official of the Army and the Interior Ministry. In the latter, he was the General Director of the Division in charge of supporting African National Liberation movements. He took part in guerrilla warfare together with Ernesto Che Guevara in Congo-Leopoldville and appeared in war zones with Al-'Asifah Palestinian commandos against Israel in the Jordan River banks.

Ulises Estrada Lescaille was the first deputy chief of the Americas Department of the Party's Central Committee, a right hand of its chief, Commander Manuel Piñeiro, known at the time as "Red Beard", who was a member of the Central Committee, but also supported the Intelligence work for Latin America leading the area's penetration and subversion.

Ulises, a tall Black man, with a totally shaved head, quiet demeanor and good manners, known for some CIA's close circles as 'the Black Panther", served as ambassador in Jamaica, Democratic Yemen, the Democratic Arab Sahrawi Republic, and Algeria,

Besides being Director of North Africa and the Middle East in the Foreign Ministry, he was also the Director of the Non-Aligned Countries' Movement Division and Deputy Minister.

Starting in 1990, he was the head of information of the daily *Granma,* the party's official organ, and Director of the Tricontinental magazine of the Asian, African, and Latin American Countries' Solidarity Organization.

Shortly before leaving overseas, the Counterintelligence (DGCI) of the State Security recruited me.

For some time, I held several secret meetings in a "contact house", where a female official dressed as a civilian would read a small instruction book. First of all, the first objective of the State Security was to protect the life of the then Commander-in-Chief, Fidel Castro, for which any hint of information regarding any attempt against his life had to be reported immediately. I used the pseudonym "Javier" and I was tasked with routine checkup and information search among diplomats accredited in Havana with whom I worked with.

Also, with the same end, I had to report on topics of interest, previously stated in a guide, on talks I had with foreign delegations I attended to when visiting Cuba to take part in international events.

Yasser Arafat, PLO Chairman, first visited Cuba on November 14th 1974, a day after having delivered a speech in the UN General Assembly in New York.

I remember that with a month left for graduation, I was asked together with a classmate of mine, due to our Arab physical resemblance, to dress up with suit and tie ready to work for an Arab delegation. We went to the Ministry's Press and Culture Division, where we had been summoned, and the director told us to be near at hand. My partner and I headed to the Riviera Hotel which was near the Ministry, and sat by the swimming pool to drink a Cuban typical drink: mojito. At that time, my friend, Roberto Blanco, who later was appointed ambassador, and I, wore moustaches.

In a table nearby, several Arabs stared at us, looking visibly uneasy. One of them got up and entered the hotel lobby. We finished our mojitos and returned to the Ministry to check whether we were needed. Then we were told that Yasser Arafat's personal security, whose delegation coincidentally was staying at the Riviera Hotel, something we were unaware of, had contacted the Cuban security inquiring about my friend and myself, since we had looked suspicious in the pool area due to our Arab looks.

Finally, for other reasons, we were not needed there, so we went back to the Institute. But who would say at that time that ten years later, we would personally meet in Damascus with PLO Chairman, Yasser Arafat, and we would have direct contact and relations with Palestinian organizations for seven years.

As a result of Arafat's visit to Cuba, a "PLO Delegation" was set up in Havana, which worked as any other diplomatic embassy.

As time went by, as a Foreign Ministry official, things paved the way for the enigmatic, attractive, and sometimes dangerous Foreign Service, where diverse traditions, cultures, politics, interests, subtle deceits, undercover operations, and dark personalities would become part of my mission abroad.

My first assignment after carrying out a specific training plan within the Ministry and other state bodies, was that of Third Secretary of the Cuban Embassy in Damascus, Syria.

The Middle East was a strategic region in the world, not only for its economic and commercial value, but also for its strategic geographic and military location because of the access to the Arab-Persian Gulf and serve as a bridge between Europe, Asia, and Africa.

The region, very rich in history, religion, and mythology, is involved in legendary border, political, ethnic, and religious disputes; territorial occupation, geographic and ideological divisions. Besides, it has been part of several empires, crusades, open wars, and undercover operations of all kinds.

Many analysts have predicted that if, unfortunately, a Third World War took place, it would begin in the Middle East Conflict, a place that was the cradle of civilization, land of Jesus Christ, Moses, and Mohammad. It is a sacred region turned into the apple of discord, where the three most influential religions in the world are intertwined.

The United States, after overthrowing Saddam Hussein in Iraq, found itself stagnated for a few years in an attempt to stabilize that country but, at the same time, remained at war with terrorists in the region, including Afghanistan. That situation turned into an endless nightmare.

For its part, the Iranian Islamic regime, due to its oil wealth, vast territory, a large population, and a profound religious fanatism, could become a regional superpower. Iran continued to try to develop its nuclear military program and has received several warnings by the United States.

The final objective of the Islamic Republic of Iran is to convert the whole planet to Islam and subdue all those who are not Muslims, since, for them, the latter represent Satan.

For the so-called Muslim countries, including Iran, which is Persian, not Arab, religion goes beyond faith and beliefs, it embodies a form of life present in their traditions, morals, economy, politics, and laws.

47

Sharia, which literally means "road to a water fountain" is the Muslim law inspired in Islam, which is not refutable as Quran is, and is a mandatory, detailed code of conduct. Within Muslim Sharia, there is a type of offense known as "Hadd", which is crimes punished with harsh sentences such as stoning, whipping, one-hand amputation, and hanging. Not all Muslim countries apply these sentences the same way.

In seven countries practicing Sharia (Sudan, Iran, Saudi Arabia, Mauritania, Pakistan, Afghanistan, and Yemen), homosexuality is punished with whipping and even the death penalty. In the Islamic countries, the death penalty is carried out through beheadings, stoning, or hanging. In Saudi Arabia, for example, convicted individuals are beheaded with a sword cutting their neck. They also cut thieves' hands off, and practice stoning.

Stoning, also used in countries such as Iran, Iraq, and the United Arab Emirates, consists of burying a man's half body, and a woman up to the neck. Then, they are thrown rocks and stones of different sizes until they die in about thirty minutes.

Hanging is also used, like the one applied to former Iraqi President, Saddam Hussein, when he was executed.

I personally saw the hanging in a public square in Damascus of an individual, who had raped and killed a woman. They can also be sentenced to hang for killing or stealing.

The existence of so strong sentences, misdeeds or crimes have quite declined. I can mention as an example that, during my stay in Syria, I could leave my car open and the windows down and nothing would happen. If we forgot to pick up merchandise already paid for at the market, the merchants would come after us calling to hand us the forgotten items. Stealing was almost non-existent.

The policy used by Muslim merchants trying to make money in their sales is by asking for excessive prices, which leads to "bargaining", but this is legal and a popular tradition.

CHAPTER III

ARRIVAL IN DAMASCUS

1976

"Marhaba, ahla wasahla", we were greeted and welcomed in Arabic during our first arrival at the old Damascus International Airport on December 16th, 1976.

Several beggars reached out asking for a charity, "Massari" (money); others were sitting and kneeling on small rugs praying the Quran. Women wore the typical "Hijab" (Islamic veiling) similarly known in a more modern style as "Shayla". Some also wore the black tunic or "Chador", which covers almost all the body down, bracelets, and gold rings. Many dressed Western style but discreetly.

Syria is one of the most "Progressive" Arab countries as far as women's clothing is concerned.

Many men with beards and moustaches donned the "thobe", an Arab tunic or attire; others the "Guthrie", a red and white-striped headdress with a black cord around the head; the "Shemaghs" Arab scarfs or the Palestinian "Kaffiyeh" type. But also, a great deal dressed the Western way.

The signs written in Arabic from right to left looked in our eyes as a sort of hieroglyphics. There was a crowd making a noise we could not understand, plus a strong smell of food cooked with lamb fat and a lot of spices. As it is known, by

50

religion and tradition, Arabs prefer to eat sheep meat or beef as a second choice, since eating pork is forbidden by Islam. I thought that we had indeed arrived in a world quite different from ours as expected.

-"Comrade Aguililla", someone called me.

"Yes, what is it?" I responded.

"My name is Antonio Torres, but you can call me Tony. I'm the Cuban Embassy administrator".

Tony held the rank of diplomatic attaché. I had already been informed that he was the trustworthy man of the Ambassador, and that is why he worked the finance section. He was a short person with white skin and brown hair and eyes.

"Tony, let me introduce you to my wife, Miriam Rodriguez Varela and my little daughter, Maitelis".

My wife, whom we affectionately called Mirita, still kept her maiden name, as it is customary in Cuba. Maitelis would turn two years old three months from that day.

After the introduction and greetings, Tony said:

"Please, give me the luggage tickets because Said, one of the native drivers will take the luggage in another car. We are going in my car".

On our way to the city, Tony asked:

"How was the trip?".

"Our first stopover was in Madrid", I answered. The taxi driver who took us from the airport to the hotel told us

51

the Spaniards were losing their jobs due to the Cuban immigrants. That there was a saying that went like this: "If you don't want to cut sugar cane, go to Spain: which made us laugh. In Madrid", I continued, "the first thing we did was to go to the store called El Corte Inglés. There we bought a new coat for our daughter because the one she had on had been made by a Cuban neighbor in Cuba with good intentions, adorned with rabbit skin, which we threw straight into a store trash can. I bought two good leather pairs of shoes, and I also dropped the one I had on in the trash can. Likewise, Mirita also took the opportunity to purchase whatever she most needed".

"Let's head to the apartment, originally occupied by Ramiro Rodriguez, previous embassy counselor, where you will reside", Tony pointed out, "but, Aguililla, keep talking about your trip".

"Of course, Tony", I added, 'In Madrid, we stayed at the Moderno Hotel, located in the city center in Puerta del Sol, where kilometer 0 lies. We stayed for just three days", I kept saying. "But during that time, we visited the Prado Museum, the Gran Via, the Royal Palace, and the Alcala Gate. We were at the hotel just to sleep. As to shopping", I kept talking while he was driving, "we also went to another store called Galerias Preciados, the shoe store 'Los Guerrilleros', and the street market known as 'El Rastro'. We also went to several restaurants, among them 'Los Montes', a small one which became well known among Cubans in transit there because of the good food and cheap prices. Of course, also a good wine or a 'caña' (a glass of beer). Likewise, I liked the 'Carajillo', a mix of coffee and brandy or cognac, good to fight cold weather. It is said that the name 'Carajillo' comes from the times when Spain invaded Cuba. When provisions started to get scarce, the Spaniards began to use native products such as coffee and rum, the mixture of which gave them 'Courage' and the usual phrase before going to combat was 'let's go get them, Carajillo'. Hence the expression 'Corajillo-Carajillo'

"By the way", Tony interrupted, "I forgot to tell you that Ambassador Barber and his wife Clarita send their regards and welcome you. They were looking forward to your arrival. The Ambassador told me, to take you to the apartment so you can settle down and rest tonight. The apartment is ready, including some food. Tomorrow", Tony continued to say, "I'll drive by to pick you up Aguililla, and take you to the embassy, but keep talking. How was Paris?

Mirita, who had remained quiet so far, plucked up courage to speak and said:

"Look, Tony, when I got to Paris, I was wearing the coat I bought in Cuba and Hectico", -that's how people close to me call me, "an overcoat borrowed from Felix Pita, a journalist friend of ours who was a counselor in Lebanon, but it was oversized. Then two of the French guards at the

53

Charles De Gaulle airport customs looked at us and whispered to themselves: 'What kind of diplomats.' But Hectico, who knows French, could hear them". Later on, Mirita continued, "in a cafeteria in Paris, Hectico complained to the waiter that the bill was somewhat high, to which the waiter answered: 'Paris is like this. You have to come here with a lot of money'. Actually, it was a rip-off", Mirita said, "for a pair of buns and two small glasses of Coca-Cola, we were charged the equivalent of $75 US dollars in an ordinary cafeteria. I got the impression that some French", she kept saying, "think they are 'the last Coca-Cola in the desert". Of course, there are also good and polite people like everywhere else. But in the end, their famous Seine River has many dirty places, and the Eiffel Tower was closed to the public for repairs. We left the Tower in a hurry to the hotel because it was snowing a lot, and it was too cold for our daughter". "Also", she added, "we saw the Arc of Triumph on the Champ Elysees' Avenue, but we didn't have time to visit the Louvre Museum, which is what I would have liked to see the most. Although I sincerely say, if it were for me, I'd never go back to France. On the other hand," Mirita said, "I loved Madrid, not only for its cultural closeness but also because I liked all the places I visited, and the people are friendlier and more polite".

Tony interrupted her and said:

"We're already in the city. The highway you see over there exiting the traffic circle goes to the newest part of Damascus, called Mezze, where the Ambassador's residence is located.

We finally arrived at the apartment, which covered the whole floor below street level, in a building on a distinguished neighborhood. It was huge: there was a small entrance hall where we hung our coats, and then there was a hallway. On the first door to the left, there was a regular hall which was connected to an office through another door. Straight at the end, the hallway reached the living room, and to the right there was a big kitchen. The living room had a door that led to a big dining room with a table for twelve guests. The hallway also had another door with access to an area with three bedrooms. In the back of the apartment, there was a large outdoor patio covered with pavers and a couple of water fountains. The patio could be reached from three different doors.

After showing us the apartment plus some food they had bought, and handing me the keys, including the one for the embassy, Tony took his leave and promised to return and pick me up the next day at 10 am. At that time, the Cuban government recommended that, we officials abroad lived in apartments to have higher security and, of course, save money. That apartment, as Tony had said, had been first occupied by former counselor Ramiro, but during the last two years, when Ramiro had returned to Cuba, it was used by the Third Secretary Sergio (Bebo) Montané Oropesa, brother of Jesús Montané Oropesa, member of the Politburo of the Cuban Communist Party's Central Committee. This Sergio evidently had in the embassy what is known in Cuba a 'bottle' (Cuban slang for 'Cushy Thing', a position obtained through his brother despite his incompetence for the job.

At dawn the following day, 6:05 am, we were woken up by a very loud noise; my first reaction was, being half asleep, to think someone had placed powerful speakers within the rooms. Then I told Mirita:

"Maybe this is a welcoming bad joke by the embassy staff although it really puzzled me.

On realizing that the noise came from outside, I went out to the balcony and discovered that there was a mosque across the street near the building. The mosque powerful speakers call the faithful and they blare five times a day to comply with as many times prayers are made daily, according to the Quran. All over the city you could hear the loud exclamation of "Alá akbar, Alá Akbar (God is Great).

Tony picked me up as promised and took me to the embassy, which was at a ten-minute drive away. There were a lot of Syrian guards with long guns near the embassy, guarding a building on the street corner facing the embassy, which was none other than the Presidential Palace of then President Hafez El Assad.

The palace was built with many columns around coupled with the typical Arabic lobed arches with a tall wall blocking the view. Cars entered the palace through a street that lay between the former and the Cuban embassy, so it was only logical that all that area was closely guarded.

Houses in Damascus were characterized by not showing a fancy façade but did have a great luxury within and in its internal large patios and gardens.

The Cuban embassy was a four-floor building with a porch surrounded by a gated wall and trees. To the right of the entrance was the main door leading to the reception desk; in the center, a wide glass French-style double door preceded by marbled steps showing the way to a protocol room; and to the left, a small private door that took you straight to the Ambassador's office. Also, to the far left, a room had been built for a small school with Cuban teachers.

Upon arriving, the Third Secretary welcomed me, Bebo Montané Oropesa, whom I would replace in the embassy staff.

"Aguililla", Bebo told me, "I was very glad to hear about your appointment in this mission. I was in charge of consular affairs, but I understand you'll take care of Palestinian affairs, Syrian foreign policy analysis, Syrian-Cuban bilateral relations, the Arab-Israeli conflict, and military affairs. I know you are well-trained for all that. Congratulations."

"Yes, I knew about it", I answered, "in a small mission, you have to do a bit of everything, ha, ha, ha, and I like being busy, I'm ready for it so I'm not worried."

Bebo continued to explain:

"The other Third Secretary, Eduardo Castellanos, will take care of assessing the Syrian domestic policy, trade and economic affairs, the press and cultural stuff. And now the consular ones I used to do."

That embassy had a peculiar characteristic: the counselor position had been removed. From the Ambassador down, the rank hierarchy consisted of just two Third Secretaries. That caused a great vacuum between the Ambassador level and the lower rank of Second in Command of the mission. Later, after learning about the egocentric personality of Ambassador Barber, I could explain to myself the reason for that particular arrangement.

An embassy staff, depending on the importance given to the country and the status of bilateral relations, may include counseling ministers; counselors, first, second, and third secretaries; and diplomatic, military, commercial, cultural, and consular attachés, besides a backup personnel made up of administrators, technicians, custodians, drivers, etc.

In the case of the Cuban embassy in Syria, the Cuban staff included an administrator; a Communications technician from the Interior Ministry, Intelligence Division, in charge to operate the radio transmissions; another technical member of the eighth Encoding Dept. from the same Intelligence Division, who encoded and decoded secret messages; a Cuban driver of the Ambassador and a personal secretary for the Ambassador; all of them with the rank of 'diplomatic attachés' in their passports to have diplomatic immunity.

Likewise, there were office secretaries, a cleaning staff, and a female teacher for the kids. Most of these positions were covered by the Cuban diplomats' spouses in the embassy. Moreover, there were other positions taken by Syrian natives, such as the receptionist, translators, and a driver for administrative matters.

Bebo and I went into Ambassador Barber's office on the first floor. The office had stylish furniture, a large desk, and then a wide two-wing door that led to the office of his personal secretary, who was also Cuban with the rank of diplomatic attaché. The secret documents were kept there.

Ambassador Arturo Barber Orozco, Extraordinary and Plenipotentiary representative of the Republic of Cuba and its head of state, then Fidel Castro, was waiting for us.

Barber was a lawyer by trade and had been deputy Justice Minister for the Cuban government. He was around fifty-five years old back then, with white hair, average height, and as a lawyer had great verbal skills. Rumors had it that his wife, Clara Velis, had played a vital role in Barber's nomination as ambassador due to her leverage in the government apparatus.

The Ambassador's wife was a native of Cienfuegos city, just like her godfather, Dr. Carlos Rafael Rodriguez, member of the PCC's Politburo, in charge of international relations and one of Fidel's closest collaborators.at the time. Clara Velis had a sister called Lupe, married to Antonio Nuñez Jimenez, also ambassador back then. Nuñez Jimenez came down from the mountains as a guerrilla fighter from Sierra Maestra (a mountain range) ranked as captain under the orders of Che Guevara; was a scientist, President of the Academy of Sciences, the National Institute of Agrarian Reform, and the Cuban National Bank.

Moreover, Clara had another sister, Esther, who was the head of the International Relations Department of the Cuban Women's National Federation, the president of which was Vilma Espín, Raul Castro's ex-wife. Anyways, the three Velis sisters were well positioned.

"Welcome, Aguililla", Barber exclaimed, "I heard you had a long trip. I'm glad you're already here. I guess Bebo already gave you the heads up about what we're going to do, but let's go to my residence so you get to know it and talk more at ease.

In the diplomatic field, there are two renown places which have guaranteed special diplomatic immunity: one is the embassy, where the work offices of the Ambassador and the accredited diplomatic officials work; and secondly, the residence, where the ambassador resides.

We said goodbye to Bebo and went out through the Ambassador's private door. We got in the black Mercedes Benz, the Ambassador's official car, driven by Cuban driver Humberto.

Humberto's wife, who was nicknamed Tatica, had the cleaning job at the embassy. There was a Syrian woman, Janet, who cooked and cleaned at the residence.

We arrived at the residence, which was one of the biggest and most sumptuous in the diplomatic corps in Damascus. At the entrance, there was a double garage door, where Barber had a navy-blue Fiat he used as a backup car; a door to a well-decorated reception room; a large dining-living room with a view to the backyard; and a huge well-equipped kitchen with a big spacious pantry. Also, you would find a gym, an office, and a library. The floor tiles and most of the walls were made of marble and stone. On the second floor, there were bedrooms, and on the third one, a couple of guest bedrooms and another protocol room for diplomatic meetings. Lastly, it had a furnished penthouse supposedly available for an official, which had never been occupied. In the backyard, one could see a swimming pool, trees and an attached roof with grapevine covering a comfortable wing, and patio furniture.

We sat in the living room, which had a bar. Ambassador Barber treated me with a Cointreau cocktail as aperitif while his Syrian cook, Janet, finished preparing lunch. It was cold but the sun still warmed a little bit. Climate in Damascus was kind of Mediterranean and semiarid, cold in winter, mainly at night, and arid and hot specially during daytime. Syria is bathed by the Mediterranean Sea, but it also has desert areas. It snows in Damascus in winter, above all in the hills and its surroundings.

The Ambassador's wife Clara had gone to our apartment to meet Mirita and Maitelis. In the meantime, her two children, Carlos and Boris, about 9 and 12 years old, were taking classes in the embassy school.

While Barber and I were having lunch, he told me:

"Aguililla, besides your responsibilities you already know about, you'll be in charge of Jordan, since, as you know, we take care of their affairs from here. But the most important thing is that you deal with everything concerning Syria's foreign relations and the Palestinian Resistance situation. We hope", he added, "to soon increase the embassy staff with the appointment of a military attaché from the Revolutionary Armed Forces Ministry (known as MINFAR in Cuba) and a commercial attaché from the Foreign Trade Ministry (known as MINCEX in Cuba). We already have the office available for them."

After we finished eating, we had a cognac shot and a cup of coffee. Later on, we returned to the embassy, which was a twenty-minute drive from the residence.

When we arrived, he invited me into a well-decorated room with valuable paintings, fine lamps, beautiful curtains, traditional-style furniture, Persian rugs, big flowerpots, sculptures, tape recorders, projectors, and TV sets. He made himself comfortable on an armchair and said:

"This is a soundproof room and I use it to meet and discuss secret information with my closest collaborators, but, eventually, I also welcome some diplomatic counterparts from other socialist countries, members of the Syrian communist party's Politburo and some high-ranking Palestinian leaders, with which I have a very reliable intelligence exchange. Well, "Barber added" let's get to the point of interest. I'm sorry I must tell you this right off the bat, but we have to urgently send the annual confidential report to Cuba in the next diplomatic mail going out on the thirty-first of this month (December). We haven't been able to draw it up for different reasons; that's why I need your help and start right away". Barber paused and continued saying: "Aguililla, I need you to specifically prepare an annual report on the Arab-Israeli conflict, the events on Syria's foreign policy, the progress of our relations between Syria and Cuba, the Palestinian Resistance situation, and, finally, conclusions and propositions I know you can do it, even though you have just arrived, because you were our counterpart in Cuba as a specialist and are aware of everything. Later on, we'll meet to discuss it and I'll do my part too, especially on the propositions. I'll give the go-ahead to send them".

The real reasons why the annual report (1976 summary) could not be sent before my arrival yet, were that Counselor Ramiro had left permanently. He was the one who carried the weight of political affairs and the incompetence of Bebo Montané, whom I was replacing in the payroll.

Former Counselor Ramiro, who was also a friend of the head of the party's Politburo's Foreign Ministry, Dr. Carlos Rafael Rodriguez (according to a nephew of the latter), was an experienced and well-trained official. However, Bebo Montané's work was not stellar, since he only dealt with consular affairs, which were very few. As I mentioned above, he had been appointed to the post thanks to the nepotism coming from his brother, Jesús Montané Oropesa, a member of the PCC's Politburo.

Clara Velis, the Ambassador's wife, held the position of "press analyst" in the payroll. To justify her salary, a public chronology of the most important news in the Syrian press was done by the political officials, including myself since my arrival in particular, the ones where Cuba was brought up. Picture clips or articles on Cuba, which were eventually translated from Arabic by embassy's translators were included.

The only one who really took care of political affairs at the time, besides the Ambassador, was the Third Secretary, Eduardo Castellanos, who, by the way, had been a classmate of mine at the Higher Institute of Foreign Relations (known as ISRI in Cuba).

"OK", I told the Ambassador, "I'll only need your authorization to have access to all confidential files. Don't worry, I'll devote full time to this task because we just have a few days left. Despite the fact that I haven't been on the field here this year, I have studied all reports from you and other missions in the area from Havana, so I think I can do it".

"Great. I knew I could count on you", added Barber. "I'm very busy with the preparations for the reception on the eighteenth anniversary of the Revolution on January 1st, and the other officials with the other topics you are acquainted with, too. Come with me", he said and entered his personal secretary's office. He opened a file cabinet drawer and handed me a Makarov pistol with two bullet magazines.

"Only the encoder and I use the 9 mm Browning", Barber clarified. The radio operator, Castellanos and you use a Makarov. It's five handguns in all. The room of the radio operator (an official from the Interior Ministry whose specialty was coding and decoding messages with ciphered words) is also soundproof and secured. There we have also six folding

AK-47's for the embassy's defense in case of extreme need Aguililla",

Barber emphasized, "I'm going to tell you this just once. I know you'll probably have other work 'commitments' but those cannot affect your main job with me because that's what you're here for".

The Ambassador was referring that way without directly saying, eventually, to the fact that he knew I would have to cooperate with the Cuban secret service but wanted to make clear that my job as a diplomatic official from the Foreign Ministry in the mission under his command, was first and foremost.

I reply, "Of course, Ambassador, have no doubt about it, I am, above all, a Foreign Ministry official', other tasks would be occasional and secondary. I'm very clear about the fact that you are the top authority in this country, so you can rest assured that I'll always know what my priorities are".

I spent the last days of the year working until late at night. I was finally able to finish the report, and the diplomatic mail was sent to Cuba. I was just twenty-three years old, and that was my first work experience overseas.

During the last few days in December, a few weeks after my arrival in Damascus, my daughter Maitelis and I got sick with a high temperature due to a virus. Mirita had to go to a pharmacy near the apartment to buy some medication, but they only spoke Arabic, so she had to make do with body language signs. We soon got well.

The diplomatic reception to celebrate the eighteenth anniversary of the "Revolution" on January 1st, 1977, could not be held until the 7th at the Damascus Meridian Hotel. I logically took the occasion to get to know personalities from the government, and the Bass Party (Party of Socialist Arab Renaissance of Syria), as well as from the diplomatic corps accredited in that capital, some Palestinians organizations, and the Syrian Communist Party.

Subsequently, I started to have frequent contacts with the several Palestinian organizations not only to get the usual political and military information of the Resistance and the regional conflict, but also because the Cuban intelligence asked to get a profile of each Palestinian leader. There were many individuals because present in Damascus and Beirut were various Palestinian organizations.

Since the Cuban embassy was small, there was no DGI intelligence center, so eventually, they asked us for collaboration. Later, with the accreditation of a military attaché, we did have the presence of an intelligence official in the embassy although, in this case, from the Military Intelligence Division.

My wife Mirita started to work as an office secretary in charge of type, file and getting diplomatic bag ready with the unclassified documents and other shipments.

Then we started to drop Maitelis off in a children's daycare center, which had been recommended by the chairwoman of the Syrian Women's General Federation. Children of high-ranking Syrian leaders attended that center.

Mirita, although born in Havana, had been raised in the city of Placetas, located in the center of the Cuban island. She was a short young woman who dressed sharply, had white reddish skin, blond hair, green eyes, and in a good mood. Frequently, people thought she was Russian or European due to her looks. Besides, the surreal image people abroad have of the Cuban population is that it is mostly made up of mestizos, mulattos, and Blacks. Nevertheless, she was always very proud to be Cuban. She has the gift of easily become the spotlight and quickly develop social relations due to her charm and spontaneous joy.

One night, I whispered to Mirita, who logically was also my confidante:

"I have some very important ideas in mind for our future, but I haven't reached a decision to discuss it yet. I wouldn't go ahead with them without you and the kid, but some other time, I will explain it to you".

We had to be careful with what we said because there could be mikes hidden despite checking and finding none. That is why I never spoke anymore about my secret intentions for a long time and Mirita, who was very discreet, did not mention it again, either. She trusted me very much and vice versa.

One Sunday, Mirita, Maitelis, and I went for a drive in order to get to know Damascus a little more in the Peugeot 504, which had been assigned to me.

The old side of Damascus was known as the oldest city in the world, which is still inhabited. It is almost six thousand years old and was named World Heritage by UNESCO in 1979 right at the time when we were there. The name Damascus comes from Aramaic meaning "water abundance".

The great Umayyad Mosque is the city's most important one and one of the world's largest. It is famous for having the Mausoleum of Saladin, Sultan of Syria, Egypt, and Palestine; the shrine with the head of Imam Husayn Ibn Ali, grandson of Prophet Muhammad; and the remains of Saint John the Baptist, who was revered there by Christians and Muslims.

That old city has narrow streets and alleys where we would hardly drive through. The city also has the "Zoco" (a typical Arab market where there are long and winding aisles full of vendors with carts and stands, others showing their merchandise in any available corner or spot, and some established merchants in small, enclosed spaces). For all merchants, "to bargain" is a habit they enjoy because it is part of their culture. They may start asking for two hundred Syrian pounds for an item and end up selling it for fifty only.

Also, there were gold markets and even illegal currency exchange. Rumor has it that the currency exchange business in the black market, the sale of used clothes brought in large bales from Europe, and big batches of used cars, belonged to Rifaat al-Assad, brother of the Syrian President, who was also the feared head of the "Mukhabarat", the repressive security forces. Moreover, Rifaat had investments in France, Spain, and other European countries.

The Al-Azm Palace was built by Pash-al-Azm, Ottoman governor of Damascus as his presidential palace in 1749. It is located near the Great Umayyad Mosque, and it is an impressive representation of ancient Damascus mansions.

What is known as "New Damascus" was laid out with roads facing frequent French-style roundabouts. Syria inherited many elements of its culture from its metropolis, including the French language, spoken by a large part of its population. That was very convenient for me, since I know French very well.

My favorite place to be, was the top of a mountain, where there was a sort of a natural viewpoint with a view to the whole city of Damascus. There, peddlers were always selling food and drinks. We would eat "Falafel" (patty-shaped fritters made of ground chickpea, drizzled with paprika),

"Shawarmas" (sandwiches made with Arab bread and lamb meat grilled in a big rotating cone), and chargrilled lamb entrails in skewers. We would have a good time, and Mirita was happy with our little daughter Maitelis next to her. We would enjoy the view and fresh air flowing over that hill.

Luckily for women, Syria was one of the most progressive countries in the Arab world as far as women's dressing was concerned. Nevertheless, "machismo", women's discrimination, and mistreatment still existed.

In the capital, some women dressed discreetly but moderately. There still were religious fanatics, old-aged women, victims of extreme Arab machismo, and Bedouins, who would wear the most traditional attires, particularly in the countryside.

We visited the old city of Maaloula, located about fifty kilometers to the northeast of Damascus. This was a small town built in a valley where Aramaic, Jesus' language, was still spoken and passed on from parent to children. The town is surrounded by rugged hills which isolate and protect it from the Syrian desert that appears on the other side, which has helped to preserve its predominantly Christian religion.

A narrow road by car leads to the top of a canyon, where one of the oldest Christian churches of the world can be found. There, in its ancient altar carved in marble, you can hear the prayer in Aramaic "Abuna di bishemaya..." ("Our

Father who art in Heaven...:) just as Jesus of Nazareth would have said it.

It is an impressive and picturesque place where some natives climb with their donkeys to the canyon covered with snow in winter.

City of Maaloula (on summertime):

1977. Malula, Syria. Town built scraped on steep rocks near Damascus. A Syrian Bedouin on the left; Mrs. Miriam

Aguililla, Author's wife; and their two children, Eddy and Maitelis.

During one of the many times we visited Maaloula, we moved a bit further away along the secluded gorge behind the canyon and got to practice shooting with my pistol. Five minutes later, armed men showed up in a Jeep, I identified myself, and they contacted their base. A few minutes later, another Jeep arrived with one of the Palestinian leaders I had known. It happened that a Palestinian Front had a training camp in that area. I was told I could keep shooting there, and they even offered to bring other weapons and ammo.

In Syria, the fact that a man walks followed by several women in line behind him draws frequent attention. The Quran allows polygamy to Muslims by pointing out..." marry all the women you like, two, three, four..."

According to Muslim law, a man may have four spouses, but must provide equally for all of them. Some mark their wives' faces with tattooed dots or symbols which denote them as his property.

There are secular countries, such as Lebanon, where polygamy is banned, and others, like Syria, where it is limited, since a man must have the consent of his first wife to have another one. Polygamy is allowed just to men. In Syria's Penal Code, article 548 stipulates that a man who catches his wife or sister in adultery, and kills her or her lover, will benefit from a criminal exemption.

In July 2009, the Syrian President amended this article by issuing a decree which changes the charges for committing a "homicide of horror" to a minimum of two years in prison.

Strikingly, in France, where polygamy is forbidden, immigrant men are allowed to keep their "out-of-the-country" laws. Some of these families receive benefits for that because the French government subsidizes them with up to more than 500 euros a month per child.

Going back to our travel stories in Syria, we visited the city of Sednayah several times, the location of which is at the top of a hill thirty kilometers from Damascus, where there is a monastery used for pilgrimage by many. We used to go there often due to its closeness to Damascus, so our daughter could play in the snow, and we could chill out. Besides, I knew the owner of a hotel at the top because he was of Cuban origin and had been by the embassy several times to renew his Syrian children's passports to avoid being drafted in Syria's mandatory military service.

Further on, we drove around several cities away from the capital aimed at getting to know the country. We went to Homs, Hama. Palmyra, Aleppo, Bosra, Tartous and Latakia. The last two have ports in the Mediterranean Sea.

Thirty kilometers east of Latakia, we visited the Castle of Chevaliers, known also as the Krak des Chevaliers, due to the fact that "Krak" means fortress in Arabic. In 2006, it was declared a World Heritage site by UNESCO, together with the Castle of Saladin, very close to the former but smaller.

The Castle of Chevaliers was built at the top of a high mountain with double walls separated by a strip full of water used during the crusades. The garrison was made up of two thousand troops and had a five-year provision of foodstuff. It is the best-preserved crusade fortress in the Middle East, which protected the pilgrims' route on their way to holy places like Jerusalem and serving as security and refuge for Europeans.

The specific mission of this castle was to ensure people's transit through the established route between the Syrian city of Homs and the Lebanese city of Tripoli in the Mediterranean. It is a military architecture beauty from the Middle Ages.

In 1142, the Order of the Hospitallers settled in the Krak des Chevaliers and in 1272, the Sultan of Egypt, Baybars, captured the fortress. At present, it is a tourist center.

Not far from there, we drove to see the ruins of Ugarit, a Canaanite city where the oldest alphabet, believed to have been created around 1,300 B.C., is found, the tablet of which is in the Damascus Museum.

We passed by the city of Mari, one of the oldest dating back to 2,700 B.C. and founded by the Sumerians in the banks of the Euphrates River; Aramean, with Byzantine ruins and a green field where the best Syrian wine is produced.

Also, we visited the city of Hama, captivating with the charming Norias or giant wheels which may have up to a twenty-meter diameter, used to move the Orontes River waters.

At city of Hama, Syria, Author Mr. Hector G. Aguililla whit his two kids, Maitelis and Eddy.

Likewise, we visited the city of Palmyra, the name of which is a version of Aramaic and means "the city of date palm trees". It lies in the Syrian desert, two hundred and forty kilometers from Damascus.

History says that in 41 B.C., Mark Antony troops seized Palmyra and the result was that in the first century, Syria became a Roman province. During a visit by Emperor Hadrian to the city, he gave the city the right to be free and changed its name to Hadriane Palmyra. Queen Zenobia established her Nabatean kingdom capital in Palmyra. She preserved its independence from the Roman besiegement and siege for six years.

In 272, the "Syrian Cleopatra" was defeated and taken captive by Emperor Aurelian. In the year 634, the city was taken by Muslims and in 1809, an earthquake destroyed it in its entirety. Palmyra was named World Heritage by UNESCO in 1980.

On our way out of the ruins of Palmyra, we came across two guards with ugly looks, unshaven and wearing awful uniforms. They made us stop our car, despite it having diplomatic plates, asking for passports, and telling us to get out of the car to be frisked. We were in the desert, a far desolate area. There was no one else around, and the bearded ones were slyly laughing when they approached the car windows and looked at the windshield with a provocative glance at Mirita.

Then, suddenly, and without handing them our passports, I stepped on the gas and drove in zigzags at high speed, telling my wife and daughter to keep their heads down.

When I looked through the rearview mirror, I could see one, the guards kneeling and aiming his long gun at us, but the other guard raised his partner's gun barrel with one hand to stop him from shooting.

Mirita was willing to take chances, sharing them with an adventurous spirit. Sometimes she jokingly said her grandmother had told her to always stand by her husband, whatever it was, in good and bad times. In a more serious tone, she said that, in the end, I had to carry out dangerous missions and the least information she got, the better it was.

We traveled to Aleppo, the second population-wise largest city after Damascus, to the north of Syria, where its historic center was proclaimed Word Historic Monument by UNESCO in 1986. We also stopped by the city of Bosra, which was a hundred forty kilometers from Damascus to the south of Syria. The city's old side was also declared World Heritage by UNESCO in 1980.

What stood out in this city were its black stones and the Byzantine ruins, a couple of mosques, the Nabatean ruins, and the Roman amphitheater. The latter dates to the second century and has a capacity for 17,000 attendees.

We also went to the Golan Heights where you could see the green plantations in Israeli colonies from the Syrian side.

Both Mirita and I had been baptized and received the First Communion as Catholics in Cuba. In Mirita's case, she also received the Sacrament of Confirmation in the church of Placetas where she grew up as a child and part of her teen years. But we had to hide our religious beliefs because at that time, the "Ideological" demands and requirements were very strict for Cuban government officials. And we were not an isolated case; for instance, Raquel, a secretary who worked for the Political Division I worked for, was about to go overseas with her husband when a statuette of the Virgin Mary was detected in her luggage and, consequently, both were expelled from the Ministry,

Years later, that policy by the Communist Party changed and was gradually loosened to the point of allowing a member of the party some years ago to be a religious person.

Many of us were forced to live under a double morale by concealing our true feelings in order to survive and try to move forward. We worked for a communist government which owned all means of production and controlled everything in the country. On the other hand, we kept up an inner self or an intimate life which rejected that system, and loved God, freedom, and democracy.

Since I was in high school and during my career I would face many internal contradictions. The communist ideology instilled in school from an early age muddled our beliefs and patriotic principles. The lack of freedom of expression and information due to the total control of the latter's media by the party, kept us ignorant of reality abroad. But earlier as a teenager, I questioned the "revolution" because of the present and future opportunities for the people, their most important issues, the lack of development, and liberties. I would realize that the system was failing.

The idea of leaving the country and abandoning the system had been taking shape in my mind more and more, although I was always curbed by the false concept wielded by the communist leaders at their whim of a false "treason to the homeland". I still had not been able to clearly comprehend that the real traitor to the homeland was Fidel Castro himself, who lied to, cheated, and manipulated the people. And it was not just that, but also the course to put back development dragging it to misery and communism under a totalitarian dictatorship which violated the most basic human rights.

After living just three to four months in the Damascus apartment, Mirita asked me to try to move because she did not like the place, because it was too big, and, besides, there had been several incidents.

One night, she saw the silhouette of a face with a moustache through the bathroom window and called me scared to death. I went out with my pistol, checked all over the backyard and the building and found only a uniformed custodian outside. I angrily showed him the pistol and told him a thing or two, which I believe he understood. He said it could have been the driver of a Syrian minister who lived next door, and who, according to the custodian, was always prowling around.

The embassy receptionist set up a courtesy visit for me and Mirita to visit our neighbors: the minister and his wife. So, we did, and we were welcomed the following day in their house in a well-decorated room which, for my liking, I found too Baroque or overloaded with art pieces. We explained to the minister what had happened and what the custodian had said about his driver. He thanked us for the visit and said he would change drivers because he was not happy with that driver either, since he had received other complaints.

Another day, Mirita called me at the embassy because someone had been banging on the main door. When I hurriedly arrived, I found there were employees from the water supply company who, after getting fed up with knocking on the door, started to turn the water off at the meter. I paid the bill while complaining about their attitude. The embassy administrator, Tony, had forgotten to pay the bill.

In the system we lived in, due to the miserable salary we earned, the government paid the diplomatic officials' lodging, including water, power, phone bills, car, and gas.

Something else Mirita disliked was that the neighbors upstairs threw their garbage down to our balcony. Besides, big, aggressive, semi-wild cats roamed our backyard threatening my little daughter when she wanted to go out there. Cats in Arab countries are sacred due to several myths and legends.

For all of the above, we moved to a new apartment on a second floor in modern Damascus, somewhat close to the Ambassador's residence.

The new apartment landlord was a Syrian called Hachem, who dealt with retail trade. His wife was a teacher and had two children.

The day we negotiated the rent and had his approval for the rent, his wife threw her wedding ring to the floor, which struck me coming from an Arab woman. He then explained to me that she had been the one who had come up with the money to buy that apartment. Finally, they came to terms and approved the deal.

One day, while working at the embassy, I got a call from the receptionist (a Syrian employee called Maha who had been working for the embassy for over twenty years) over the intercom who told me Mr. Hachem, the apartment landlord, was by the lobby, and whose daughter had body burns caused by an accident two days ago when a bucket full of boiling water fell upon her at the house. And he was coming looking for help,

A Cuban military brigade that arrived in Syria in 1973 had brought with them burn specialists to the Damascus military hospital. I rushed to the hospital and spoke with its director. I requested, on behalf of the collaboration Cuba had provided them, to give the injured girl aid. I handed him a written request on behalf of the embassy and was able to have her admitted and given free assistance. Mr. Hachem was most certainly grateful,

In Syria, seventy-five percent of the population is Sunny Muslim, but the two last presidents of the Assad family (father and son) belong to a Muslim minority sect called Alaouite, which, together with the Druze and Shiites, made up just fifteen percent of the population. The remaining ten percent are Christians.

Ramadan is held in the ninth month of the Islamic calendar. During that month, Muslims fast during the day and abstain from eating, drinking, making love, or slandering anybody. In the evenings, families gather and eat in a festive mood.

Syria lies in the region bathed by the Euphrates and Tigris rivers, where the first world civilization came into being, the area of which is called Mesopotamia. The

Euphrates is the only river that goes through Syrian territory, though.

Syria also has a very special or strategically interesting geographical location due to its borders with Lebanon, Israel, Jordan, Iraq and Turkey.

The Syrian city of Ebla was discovered by archeologists in the country's north in 1964. It was founded around 2,500 B. C. where fifteen thousand tablets with cuneiform writing in a proto-semitic language were found. The "eblaite" language is the oldest among the Semitic languages.

From the second century B.C. on, Syria was occupied by the Hittites, Canaanites, and then by the Phoenicians and Arameans. The Hebrews settled by the south of Damascus in a region called Canaan. The Phoenicians established themselves around the coastal areas and west of Lebanon.

Moreover, Syria was successively invaded by Egyptians, Sumerians, Assyrians, Babylonians, and Hittites. Later, it fell into the hands of Persians and Greeks with the conquest by Alexander the Great, and afterwards by the Romans and Byzantines. It became part of the Ottoman Empire from the sixteen to the twentieth centuries.

After World War I, in 1922, the League of Nations distributed the territories between the United Kingdom (Transjordan and Palestine) and France (Syria and Lebanon).

In 1946, Syria became independent from France and in 1958, it formed a Federation with Egypt called the United Arab Republic, which was dissolved after a military uprising in 1961.

In November 1970, the then Defense Minister, Hafez El Assad, carried out a peaceful coup d'etat and became President. Since then, he ruled Syria until 2000, when he died of a heart attack. His older son, Basil, who had been trained to succeed him, died six years before in a car accident. Thus, his second son, Bashar El Assad, who graduated as a physician specialized in Ophthalmology in London, was called.

By 1999, Bashar had already managed to make his father expel his advisor, Ali Duba, former head of military intelligence, for fear of his rivalry to the Presidency.

The Magna Carta was amended by the National Assembly the same day the death of Hafez El Assad was announced on TV in 2000.

The Bass Party Committee named Hafez El Assad's son as the new President and Commander-in-Chief of the Armed Forces; hence power passed on from father to son.

Location of Syria on the regional map:

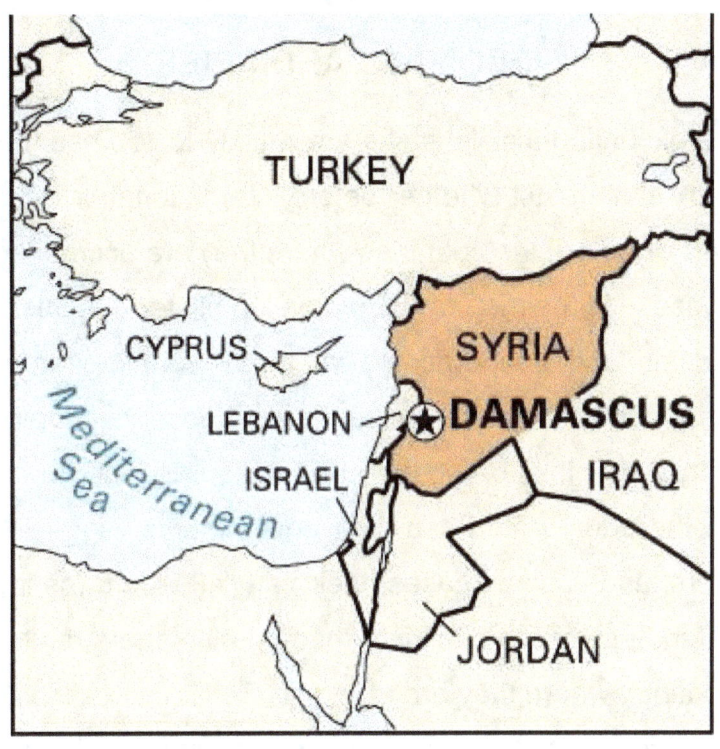

CHAPTER IV

DIPLOMATS AND SPIES

Diplomatic officials' tasks are mainly to represent their country's interests, whether before international or regional bodies or before the countries where they are accredited in. Likewise, it is their job to try to develop bilateral relations of friendship and cooperation with those countries through cultural and commercial exchange, and economic, political, military, and other branches' cooperation. But at the same time, their duty is to keep their governments' high-ranking leaders, and in some cases, their party's leaders (as it is in totalitarian societies) well informed on all matters related to the country where they are at.

In order to achieve their goals, diplomatic officials use information search techniques through public means such as the press, radio, talks in diplomatic circles, in unofficial and official meetings, but they also employ secret sources.

Furthermore, they assess the gathered information and send it in a public or confidential nature, according to the case, to their country's organization and high-ranking officials. They often include some conclusions and propositions to the highest spheres, depending on their importance.

Sometimes, given the urgency and relevance of the information, short encoded messages are sent to protect not only the info but also the sources' identities.

It is very common for most governments to use the guise of their diplomatic officials as a choice to have undercover intelligence agents in foreign countries while protected with diplomatic immunity. They also have intelligence agents who are commonly called spies, infiltrated through other means and ways. That is why diplomats and spies are well linked and have related tasks although not the same ones. Intelligence officers search for more specialized information, use more secret tools, and create profiles of persons of interest to try to recruit them as collaborators or use them as info sources. To that end, they exploit ideological affinity, friendship, and mainly sex, let alone blackmail, corruption, and bribery.

Among the circles of relationships, I established in the diplomatic corps in Damascus, was Mr. Carlos de Diego, Charge D'affaires from Panama, who I bring up as an example for the reader's interest. This Panamanian diplomat had very good connections with Latin Americans' and Spain's diplomats. Besides, Carlos also had close relations with the First Secretary of the U.S. Embassy, with whom he often used to play tennis.

From the beginning, I suspected Carlos had to have ties with the CIA, and through him, I could get some info on the

Americans. Of course, I knew they would try to do the same with me, but that was the challenge of diplomacy: to try to get important info without giving away yours or, as a last resort, to provide only the non-confidential, public and insignificant, general remarks. Carlos lived alone in the country and was always looking for company, since he was talkative and a nice person.

He was very useful for me, because he served as a bridge for me to establish good relations with Spanish-speaking diplomats, who I joined in cultural events, cocktail parties, lunch, and dinner occasions, including friendly private ones without protocol.

I could also obtain a lot of info of great interest through Carlos from his American "diplomatic friend", who was none other but the head of the CIA in the U.S. Embassy in Damascus.

Once, while visiting Carlos' residence, he told me:

"Hector, may I borrow a handgun for self-defense? You know I live alone, and you never know what may happen".

"Sure", I answered, "I'll lend you a Russian Makarov that I have temporarily available in the embassy, while you continue to offer me your collaboration, ha, ha, ha, logically".

The weapons we had at the embassy had been left by the Cuban military mission which had been secretly present in Syria during the known Yum Kippur War in 1973. That war was an operation carried out by Syria and Egypt against Israel.

I arrived in the country in December 1976. The Cuban military left Syria in February 1975. According to information received from the "Secrets from Cuba" forum, on the Cuban side, an armored brigade of T-55 tanks, a peloton of T-60 tanks, and some reactive and conventional artillery pieces, took part.

Heading such military mission was General Leopoldo Cintra Frias, who was later appointed Minister of the Cuban Revolutionary Armed Forces on November 9th, 2011.

The Cuban military secretly flew wearing suit and tie from Cuba on three TU-144 aircrafts with a stopover in the then German Democratic Republic to fill up on their way to Syria in 1973.

Syrians would give them supplies, and the technical part was handed to them by the Russians, who had advisors there.

It is said that the presence of tanks manned by Cubans in the Golan Heights helped to curb Israeli attacks.

Twenty-five years later, on October 23rd, 1998, the *Diario Las Americas* released the following in Miami:

'Havana. Breaking with a discretionary policy of a quarter of a century, the official daily *Granma* disclosed what the "second internationalist mission" the Revolutionary Armed Forces was the Syrian campaign in 1974 against the

Israeli aggression in which engaged were eight hundred Cuban tank officers.

Colonel Vicente Diaz Garcia, deputy chief of the Army political section, told the daily details of that campaign, the second one of the Cuban Army overseas, after Algeria in 1963. The story unknown to many Cubans, started in 1973 when Damascus asked Havana for military cooperation before the Israeli advance in the military conflict that began in the Middle East in 1967.

'It's in that scenario that the top authorities of that Arab nation requested Cuba the military collaboration which, at first, was with combat pilots', Diaz recalled.

Unable to send pilots to avoid neglecting its defense, Cuba proposed sending a brigade of eight hundred tank officers who traveled by air 'with absolute discretion' between October and November of 1973. After adapting the Syrian-held Russian T-54's and T-55's to the desert terrain conditions and repairing them, Cubans entered the battlefield in March of 1974.

In mid-April, we started to train the troops by sending small units to the front for fifteen days, Colonel Diaz said, who added that 'the Cuban participation consisted of involving in artillery dual engagement.

In June of 1974, a ceasefire agreement was reached between Israel and the Arab countries. The Cubans went back to their surveillance positions until February of 1975, when they returned to Havana'.

I actually had no pistol left available from the ones that had been left by the Cuban military at the embassy after leaving for Cuba, but one of our diplomatic attachés was on vacation in Havana and I had his pistol in a safe. I thought I had time before he came back to get another one, and the Panamanian Charge D'affaires would be grateful and committed to me, which is what I was interested in.

Right away, I sent an encoded message to Commander Manuel Piñeiro, better known as 'Red Beard' or 'El Gallego' (the Galician), who headed the Americas' Department of the PCC's Central Committee, which served as support to the General Intelligence Division. I asked him for a pistol and the go-ahead to lend it to the head of the Panamanian mission. Nevertheless, the next day I gave Carlos the one I kept, which was assigned to the attaché on holidays knowing I was taking a dangerous risk.

A few days later, Carlos told me that his U.S. colleague had given him a Smith & Wesson and, sarcastically showed me both Guns telling me:

"Now I have both a Russian and an American pistol. Life is full of surprises!

"Be careful", I replied, "You are playing with a double-edged sword, and it's dangerous". I capitalized on that and took the Makarov pistol from his hand and added: "I'm glad you have a good gun; you don't need mine".

So, that confirmed my suspicions that the relationship between Carlos and the American diplomats was that of collaboration with the CIA and that Carlos wanted to play the game of double agent.

Commander Manuel Piñeiro responded by encoded message from Havana that it was not convenient to lend the weapon to the head of the Panamanian mission because he was a close friend of President Manuel Noriega. I did not really fully understand his point, but whatever it was, I had already recovered the pistol I had given to Carlos and had it back in the embassy.

Manuel Noriega was the chief of Intelligence in Panama under the presidency of Omar Torrijos until August of 1983, when he took over the National Guard, and carried out a purge and placed trusted men all over the government, army, embassies, and consulates. Noriega established an unprecedented alliance with Fidel Castro, including intelligence information exchange, illegal trade operations, support for insurrections, and narco-trafficking.

Noriega worked for the CIA since he was a student. He conveyed information to Castro on the United States and vice versa. On the one hand, he aided Fidel in sending weapons to the Sandinistas, and on the other hand, he served as a link for the aid the United States was giving the Nicaraguan contras.

In 1989, Noriega was detained and taken to the United States. In 1992, he was put on trial and sentenced to forty years in jail on the charge of being related to the Medellin cartel. The sentence was later reduced, but since 2007 he was in a Miami jail waiting to be extradited to France accused of money laundering, the extradition taking place in April of 2010. In 2013, he was extradited to Panama, where he was sentenced to sixty years. Known in his country also as "Pineapple Face" due to the marks left by acne, he died in 2017 of a brain hemorrhage.

In Damascus, the Panamanian Charge D'affaires, behaved even more cooperative, which I obviously took advantage of. We were so close that, on occasions, I helped him draft and send telexes to his foreign ministry quarters from his office.

Likewise, we went on excursions to the mountains and cabaret shows together in the Meridian and Sheraton hotels. From time to time, we had lunch, dinner and even breakfast in restaurants, our houses, or in those of the Spanish-speaking diplomats.

Carlos provided me with a lot of info on his conversations with Western countries' diplomats and, especially the American. He even drew a sketch of the U.S. Embassy interior.

(See Mr. Carlos in the middle in the photo below)

1983. Damacus, Syria, Diplomatic Recepction.
Left to righ: Author, Mr. Hector G. Aguillla, Cuban
Charge D'Affair a.i.; Mr.Carlos, Charge D'Affairs of
Panama; and Lt. Col. Miguel Barreiro, Cuban Military
Attahe.

Among the plans of the 'Special Period', called like this because allegedly the Cuban economy was redesigned, and a great deal of the government work was restructured after one of the major crises. According to the Colonel Labrador, head of Dept. One (Military Intelligence office) within the Foreign Ministry, and General Luis German Barreiro, chief of intelligence, in case of a general military blockade to Cuba or a military attack where all communications of Cuba with the outer world were cut off, we had to attack with the available means the U.S. Embassies of the countries where we were stationed. Also, we had to act independently, even on an autonomous basis if needed.

As a support for that alleged scenario, General Barreiro confidentially reported that secret accounts were being opened abroad on behalf of Fidel.

Later, I learned that General Barreiro, head of intelligence, was referring to the 'Havana International London Bank' known also as 'Havin Bank Ltd.', created in London under the ownership of the Cuban government and other numerous secret bank accounts, as well as corporations which were established in many countries, with some of them called tax havens.

Fidel Castro's personal wealth was calculated by Forbes magazine in 2017 in US$ 900 million, but several sources afterwards mentioned figures ranging from twelve hundred to fifteen million US dollars.

All the strategy of the so-called special period was nothing but a justification for Fidel's excessive ambitions. At the same time, he used, as usual, the pretext of an alleged aggression by the United States in order to dodge the attention off domestic issues.

Carlos, the Panamanian aforementioned, introduced me to the Ambassador of Chile, a country with which Cuba had no diplomatic relations. The Chilean Ambassador happened to be conspiring against his then president, Augusto Pinochet, since he had a brother who was a colonel in the Chilean army trying to stage a coup d'etat. He even furnished me with information on how to get their encrypted codes to be used by the Cuban intelligence.

By then, the Third Secretary, Eduardo Castellanos, was briefed to return to Cuba and I took over his job related to all political, economic, cultural, and consular affairs.

I also had to take over the care of young Cuban students we had in Damascus, studying at the Institute of Arabic Language for Foreigners, who were boarded at the university campus.

First, there were three young female Cubans: Miriam, Gisela, and Mayra, learning Arabic to become translators. After they finished their courses, they were replaced by seven young men to study Arabic in 1981, who were also boarded at the Damascus University campus.

Among those seven young men, there were two sent by the General Intelligence Division; two by the Foreign Trade Ministry, one by the Foreign Ministry, and two by the Communist Youth League (known as UJC in Cuba).

The student sent by the Foreign Ministry was Orlando Requeijo Gual, who graduated years after me at the Higher Institute of Foreign Relations.

Finally, a Military, Navy, and Air attaché; and a Commercial attaché set up offices for the first time in the Cuban Embassy in Damascus; they eased my responsibilities a bit. However, I was the mission's second in charge and, therefore, with the Ambassador in absentia, I was in charge of the embassy as Charge D'affaires, a.i.

The most important info sources we had in the diplomatic corps were the monthly meetings we held with the socialist countries' embassies on different topics.

Those meetings were very fruitful to draw up the monthly assessment reports on Syria and the situation in the region, since the members of the socialist bloc shared detailed results of most of their analysis and confidential information on political, economic-commercial, cultural, and military issues.

We worked from 9 a.m. to 4 p.m. at the embassy. Nonetheless, I was occasionally invited to cocktail parties in midafternoons and receptions at night. Mirita was sometimes invited by the diplomatic corps' ladies for tea in the afternoon, and, besides, she went with me to some receptions at night.

The embassies of all the countries represented in Syria also held receptions on their national holidays, generally their independence anniversary. This implied that very often, we had to attend diplomatic events, all of which was used to get information. Likewise, for that purpose, I scheduled two meetings a day with Syrian and Palestinian authorities, plus communist parties' leaders or members of the diplomatic corps.

Since Mirita worked at the embassy, we left Maitelis in a daycare center recommended by the Syrian protocol, because many Syrian top leaders had their children enrolled and was sponsored by the Syrian Arab Women's Federation.

Unfortunately, one day we were coming back from the embassy in the afternoon, and Mirita got off the car to pick Maitelis up as usual, but to my surprise, she got back without the kid and said:

"Hectico", as I was affectionately called, "our daughter is nowhere to be seen in the daycare center and in the morning, I handed her over to the principal herself".

"Were you able to talk with the principal?" I asked.

"No, she's not there. She's already gone home", Mirita said weeping.

I got out of the car, entered the daycare center, and made a thorough search. I went to the backyard and found a little house used maybe for storage, and I kicked the door down. Afterwards, I checked all the surroundings and was left empty-handed. I told Mirita:

"I'm going to the principal's house' wait for me here just in case there is news".

A teacher from the embassy's school, Ramon, had just arrived in a car driven by the Syrian driver, Ahmat, who, on their way pass the daycare center, stopped to know what was going on. Ramon, the teacher, worked at the embassy' school when Maitelis was still not eligible to attend due to her early age.

Ramon joined me in the car to see the daycare center's principal. I was driving at high-speed dodging traffic so much that Ramon had his hands glued up on the car roof, and his eyes were goggling but kept silent.

On arriving at the principal's house, she could only tell us that she knew nothing, and repeated the usual Arabic word "Malish", which was a conforming expression and the non-literal meaning of which is like "do not worry", "what are you going to do", "it's destiny", "that's how Allah wanted it".

I realized I could not clearly get anything from her and went back to the daycare center at high speed to report to the police.

On the way back, it came to my mind that two days ago, I had had a meeting with a Belgian diplomat who I assumed had links to the CIA, and that at that time, many Belgians traveled to Lebanon as mercenaries trafficking weapons. I already had the feeling I had made an indiscreet remark because I had told the Belgian diplomat I had a daughter in such daycare center amid our conversation. Then something crossed my mind, which I think I really would not have done: "If my daughter is not found, I'll go for an AK-47 at the embassy and the first thing I'm going to do is pay a visit to the Belgian diplomat; then I'll go to the American Embassy".

I sputtered that wild thought due to the helplessness and despair over my missing daughter in a foreign country, and for having in my subconscious the negative doctrine I had

100

been instilled against "the alleged perpetual danger of our criminal enemy: the CIA".

When I finally got back to the daycare center, Mirita was in a very angry mood, insulting the Syrian female staff, who also only knew to tell her: "Malish, Malish".

Then the embassy driver, Ahmat, approached me and told me:

"Mr. Aguililla, I spoke with a police officer who is two blocks from here, and told me they found a little girl, seemingly a foreigner, walking down the street and took her to a police station nearby".

"Thanks, Ahmat, I'll follow you in my car, let's go to the station right away".

When we arrived at the police station, a five-minute drive, I got out of the car and found Maitelis sitting by the station entrance door holding a toy, a puss in the boots, laughing unaware of everything. Ignoring the police officer, I raised her in my arms and took her to Mirita in the car, who happily hugged her. We really went through an indescribable tense situation.

Later on, I drafted a protest notice to the Syrian Foreign Ministry's Protocol Division and met with its protocol chairman.

Also, our Ambassador's wife, Mrs. Clara Velis, upon our request, met with the President of the Syrian Women's Federation to express our complaint.

Due to the above, all the staff in the daycare center were sanctioned to work in the countryside fields.

Consequently, Mirita spent some time looking after Maitelis at home without working until the latter eventually reached the age to be admitted in the Cuban school.

Another interesting anecdote was what happened during one of my scheduled meetings with a French diplomat at his embassy. In the middle of our conversation, he received a phone call and excused himself to answer, turning to me later:

"I have been informed that Tony Frangieh, his wife Vera, and their two daughters have just been murdered. It seems the executioners were members of the Lebanese Falangist forces".

I was impressed by seeing that the French diplomat had been briefed about so quickly. Tony was the son of former Lebanese president Suleiman Frangieh and led an armed militia called the

Brigade, Marada (Rebel), or Liberation Army of Zgortha, which operated in the city of Tripoli and Northern Lebanon. The Frangieh has good relations with the Syrians and fought the Falange forces of the Gemayel family, allies of Israel, in what had already become a civil war.

A few weeks later, the French diplomat called me, asking to reciprocate the visit. When we were talking, I got a phone call from Mirita, who was at home, telling me she had heard a loud explosion and there was a lot of smoke coming from the newspaper Al Bass's headquarters, which happened to be located near our house. She also heard sirens and alarms from firefighter trucks and police cars.

Then, after hanging up, trying to impress the French diplomat, I told him:

"Sir, I've just been informed that fifteen minutes ago, there was an attack with explosives on the headquarters of Al Bass, the official daily of the Bass Party, in New Damascus, apparently by the Hezbollah's Islamic pro-Iranian forces opposed to the Syrian military presence in Lebanon".

I certainly did not tell the French diplomat that the source of the information had been my wife, and because, at that time, several attacks with bomb cars had taken place in Syria, I claimed it as very likely. And I had been right.

The French was indeed amazed by how quickly "A Source" had reported the incident, just like what had happened to me in his office with the news of Tony Frangieh's assassination, so we got even.

A few weeks later, Ambassador Barber told me he had received a report from the Interior Ministry's Communication Department, stating that they had sent a new radio plant for the embassy in a Cuban ship carrying sugar to Syria. The plant we had at that time was very old and broke down frequently, which implied overspending and security risks

103

when using the telex every time the plant broke down. Such ship would arrive at the Latakia port in the Mediterranean coast in two days.

"Aguililla", the Ambassador approached me, "the paperwork in this country to register the new radio plant is long and complicated because it has to be green-lighted by the Defense and Foreign Ministries. I need you to go and bring it straight to the embassy and manage at best you can without compromising me and without putting the load in danger since it is very valuable".

"Alright. I'll only need a driver, use the embassy's van, and several cigar boxes. You'll see I'll bring that radio plant here", I answered.

The next day I left with the Syrian driver, Ahmat, to Latakia's port two hundred sixteen miles to the northwest of Damascus. There I used Ahmat several times as interpreter, since he had learned a lot of Spanish during the years he worked for the embassy. As soon as we reached Latakia, I started to get in touch with several port and customs officials. I spoke with them about the relationship between Cuba and Syria, and I gave each top official a valuable Cuban export cigar box, which were well quoted anywhere in the world. I eventually obtained a document authorizing the transfer of the commodity to the capital's customs office, which allowed me to legally take it out from the port.

I stayed in a hotel and the next day; I got into the port and boarded the ship. There I met the Cuban captain, who showed me all the ship and invited me to his cabin to have a couple of very cold beers, an aperitif, and listen to good music.

The captain told me:

"Comrade Aguililla, when we weigh anchor and leave this port, we can unload the two boxes on a boat in a place near the coast, where you can pick them up. We've done it before".

"No Captain", I replied, "It is neither necessary nor convenient to enter them illegally. I obtained an official document allowing me to transfer them legally to the capital's customs office. So, once I take them out of there, I'll bring them directly to the embassy, where we are covered by diplomatic immunity. There, we'll be able to do the necessary paperwork to make it legal, since it is legal for a mission to have that kind of equipment, as long as the host country is provided with the frequencies with which it's going to work, Plus it's specifications. No worries, captain. Everything is under control".

"Perfect, as you say, Comrade Aguililla. Now we can have lunch in my dining room", added the captain amiably.

"Great", I said, "but before I'd like to ask you a favor. I need to send to Cuba some personal items that I brought with me. Do you think it would be possible?

"No problem at all", replied the captain. "I'll declare them as part of my personal belongings, and it'll be a pleasure for me to bring them myself to your house. Leave me your address and phone number. I'll do it with pleasure", added the captain affably.

As excess baggage by plane is expensive due to the flight distance, some of the embassy staff, including myself, took these occasional opportunities to send personal stuff.

I remember once, we sent several mattresses and even some Russian washing machines in a Cuban ship; we had bought them at a good price from the Russian commercial attaché. The parcels were later picked up by relatives in Havana's harbor customs office. Even when Mirita was in Havana expecting our son Eddy, I sent her a stroller through the captain of another ship so she could use it during her trip back Havana-Damascus with the kids.

After we enjoyed a good dinner in the captain's dining room, I thanked him for his kindness and asked him to unload the boxes, because I had to part for the embassy that night.

They managed to place one wooden box containing part of the equipment in the van and the other one on the van roof, although it was a bit overloaded. I drove carefully on the way back to Damascus. We arrived at the embassy in the wee hours. The Presidential Palace guards facing the embassy did not suspect anything wrong about the van with diplomatic plates they were already acquainted with. Despite the cargo, there were no mishaps. The van stayed parked there until the embassy gate was opened at dawn.

Sometime during the morning, the boxes were unloaded, and the plant was installed in the radio operator's room on the embassy's fourth floor. Later, the Ambassador did all the final paperwork to make it legal. He even personally met with the Syrian Defense Minister.

The Foreign Ministry Economic Division instructed the Ambassador he had to cut corners on rent due to budget cuts. And since he did not want to give his mansion up, he asked me to move to his residence penthouse, which had been unoccupied so far. Thus, he spared my apartment's rent and could continue to enjoy his expensive and luxurious residence.

I moved with my wife and daughter to the residence penthouse. It was spacious, well-furnished, and decorated. There was a balcony with a nice view of the city, which was great for diplomatic events. Besides, since it was part of the Ambassador's residence, I benefited from diplomatic immunity twice.

Shortly after, Ambassador Arturo Barber Orozco received orders to leave and return to Cuba for good. He had overstayed the average time of five years that an ambassador remains in a mission in a country considered as having good and stable living conditions.

That news heartened me because I did not feel comfortable having Barber as boss for several reasons. Due to his egocentric personality, I remained to be the second in command, who was the Third Secretary of the embassy staff, which was not seen well because when the Ambassador left, heading the embassy as the mission chief was a low-ranking diplomat. This temporary substitute is called Charge D'affaires a.i.

I had to take care of the Ambassador's farewell process that lasted about three months, and then another three more months on standby to welcome and introduce the new Ambassador, who was former minister, Lester Rodriguez Perez, ex-combatant of the July 26 Movement and the Sierra Maestra with Fidel Castro.

When I acted as Charge D'Affaires a.i. (head of the embassy), waiting for the arrival of the new ambassador, I had to organize and present a reception on the occasion of a new anniversary of the attack on the Moncada garrison. The reception turned out to be funny, because before it started, I suggested to Mirita, who did not speak French:

"When the guests come in and shake hands greeting us, you tell them "Bonsoir" and when they leave at the end of the reception, you shake hands and say, "Au revoir".

"Yes, of course, it's very easy", she said and started to practice in a low voice what she had to say.

When the guests started to arrive, I realized some of them looked at Mirita puzzled, so I asked her what she was telling them. Then she answered:

"I'm telling them what you told me to tell them, "Au revoir", isn't it so?"

"No, honey, it's the other way around, ha, ha, ha, you were telling them good night. Please, you should say "Bonsoir" when they arrive".

We looked at each other and both laughed, and she never made a mistake again. More than forty years later, we still remember that and laugh.

In 1983, the famous Cuban prima ballet dancer, Alicia Alonso, Director of the Cuban National Ballet, accompanied by a ballet group, visited Syria as part of cultural exchanges between both countries.

I'll never forget that I proposed Alicia give a performance at the Damascus Sheraton Hotel Cabaret, where we would get a good financial deal, and she responded visibly upset that she was neither Sonia Calero nor a cabaret dancer. (Sonia Calero was a very good Cuban popular dancer but not a ballet dancer),

In agreement with the Syrian Ministry of Culture, we arranged an Alicia's performance in the Roman amphitheater in the Syrian city of Bosra, which amazingly still stands and has a capacity for seventeen hundred spectators. That Syrian city lies near the border of Syria and the Jordanian Hashemites Kingdom.

In another event with one of Alicia's top dance partners in old Damascus, the wife of one of the attending Syrian ministers, raised her hands several times, showing displeasure, seemingly offended by the sexuality expressed by the couple during their performance, but that never became a formal protest and the issue never had major implications.

Alicia and her companions also visited the Syrian city of Palmira. Sometimes after her return to Cuba, she made a Photography exhibition about that city in the Cuban province of Pinar del Rio, where she demanded to safeguard the historic city of Palmira then at the hands of the Islamic State terrorists.

Before Alicia Alonso left Syria, I threw a cocktail party at the terrace of my penthouse residence in her honor. Attending were members of the diplomatic corps, the Syrian Communist Party, the Palestinian Resistance, and the Cuban embassy staff. Afterwards, pleased with her visit, Alicia traveled via Spain to Cuba.

***1983, Damascus, Syria, Diplomatic Cocktail at the
Author's residence.***

Left to right: The Author, Mr. Hector G. Aguililla, Cuban
Charge D'Affairs a.i.; Mrs. Alicia Alonso, Cuban Prima
Ballerina and Director of the Cuban National Ballet; Mr.
Simon, Mrs. Alicia's assistant and husband; and Mrs. Miriam
Aguililla, Author's wife.

According to the Syrian Protocol, every time a Head of
State visited Syria, the Syrian President invited all heads of
missions of the diplomatic corps to welcome the former at
the airport. We would stand in line down the runway

welcoming the visitors and, later, would attend a huge banquet with the President.

As Charge D'affaires a.i, I attended two or three ceremonies of this kind in the absence of the Ambassador. I was driven in the official car of the mission chief, a black Mercedes Benz with the Cuban flag on a small flagpole in front of the car and was seated in the back seat.

I remember that one of the visitors I welcomed was the then President of Libya, Muammar Gaddafi, who had always been an extravagant character. His personal bodyguards were women only, with military uniforms and submachine guns.

The banquet took place in a big protocol room of the President's residence. The driver dropped me off at the entrance, and I was welcomed by the Protocol chief, who ushered me to the assigned table and seat. The number of exquisite dishes served by the waiters was very diverse. In the balcony on a second floor facing the big hall, there was an orchestra playing during dinner.

If the visiting President did not bring his wife with him, guests' wives were not invited to the banquet. That is why Mirita only accompanied me once.

Every year the Damascus International Fair was held. Cuba participated with a pavilion. The Foreign Trade Ministry and the Commerce Chamber always sent a representative in charge of setting up the exhibit and managing the pavilion.

We rented the place beforehand and dealt with all the necessary paperwork.

A small bar was always assembled within the pavilion promoting Havana Club rum and Cuban export juices such as guava and mango. Sometimes a cigar maker came from Havana to show how to manually make cigars and offer the visitors cigar samples.

During the fair, I would take the occasion to organize two or three diplomatic events in the Cuban pavilion by inviting some diplomats, Syrian officials or Palestinian leaders with whom I had a close relationship.

The new Ambassador, Lester Rodriguez, was a "political appointment" because he was not a career diplomat, but rather made one in a rush.

Unlike Barber, who had procured his appointment through his wife's influence, Lester, who, was particularly removed from office as Light Industry Minister, was assigned there to keep him far away from the regime, neutralize him, and keep him happy at the same time.

Lester Rodriguez was an early collaborator of Fidel Castro in the July 26 Movement and took part in the Moncada garrison attack. When fighting with Fidel in the Sierra Maestra mountains, he was named the latter's delegate in Miami; that is why he left Sierra Maestra and went to Miami tasked with getting and sending weapons to the Cuban guerrilla.

Together with his wife, Marcia Cespedes, also a member of the July 26 Movement, they got involved in the renown kidnapping of then famous Argentinian car racer, Juan Manuel Fangio in Havana in 1958, with the purpose of drawing attention to and making the movement's activities known at an international level; the movement would succeed shortly afterwards.

Lester had the rank of captain when the revolution triumphed. He was second in charge of the Technical Department of Investigations (known as DTI in Cuba), which was a security repressive body during the early years of the revolution. He later became Minister of Light Industry.

One of the reasons considered to appoint him as Ambassador in Damascus, besides his dismissal as minister, was his experience in arms trafficking.

Once I accompanied Lester to the dentist, and when leaving the dentist office he commented:

"Fidel dismisses and appoints in government whomever he wants".

This slip of the tongue, in my opinion due to the influence of the anesthesia applied to him, made very clear and explicit his discontent. If that comment had reached Fidel's ears, he surely would have dismissed him again, in this case as ambassador.

In order to fulfill the tasks assigned to Lester, which involved me directly for being his right hand and personally knowing the Palestinian leaders on the field, I started to reach out to the most extreme Palestinian organization with Marxist orientations. The objective was to get a hold of some special weapons requested by Havana. Next, we would start sending them to Cuba off the records. They had to be Western-made so to avoid compromising neither Cuba nor its socialist bloc allies, wherever they would be used later.

The arrival of Lester forced me to be by his side most of the time, not only for the presentation of his Letters of Credence, but also for his introduction to the diplomatic corps and the progress of his subsequent work. This happened because the appointed Ambassador Lester did not know of diplomatic customs, most of the protocol norms and procedures, as well as the internal operations of an embassy. I practically became his counselor.

Lester would ask me to join him in his official car with his driver to his diplomatic events and meetings; besides, I occasionally did some interpretation in French for him.

On repeated occasions, we met the Palestinians in the afternoons, and then he would get in my car so I would drive him to meetings. I had to take down notes, draft minutes, and even write some urgent encoded cables about those meetings.

I must recognize Lester was a good leader and treated the staff well; he was available all the time. He also had a special personality and intuition for conspiracies, which was in keeping with the relations with Palestinians and other political organizations.

Shortly afterwards, a message from the Division of Cadres and Personnel arrived, stating I had been promoted to Second Secretary and that I would take the vacant position of First Secretary in the staff. Then what Lester did was accredit me before the Syrian government and the diplomatic corps as First Secretary, which improved the vacuum in the chain of command I referred to above.

With the presence of Ambassador Lester Rodriguez and the new Military, Naval, and Air Attaché, Lieutenant Colonel Miguel Barreiro, we started to hold meetings very early in the mornings to read and analyze the daily news.

The meetings were held in my office, and on my way to the embassy, I would pick up the Cuban student sent by the Foreign Ministry, Orlando Requeijo, so he could take part in them before going to his Arabic class. In addition to that, I explained to Requeijo some daily procedures and tasks, but in a limited way because I never received either any instructions or specific plan for his training or clearance to have him get access to classified information.

Requeijo was a young man who had a good cultural background and mastered French. He graduated from the High Institute of International Relations in Cuba three or four generations after mine. Once he finished his courses on Arabic in Syria in 1986, he had a skyrocketing career. He started working as a specialist for the Division of North Africa and the Middle East in the Foreign Ministry. Soon he was appointed Ambassador of Cuba in Qatar from 1994 to 1998; Director of Foreign Ministry North Africa and Middle East Division from 1998 to 2001; Ambassador and Permanent Representative of Cuba before the United Nations from 2004 to 2006; Deputy Minister of Foreign Relations for Foreign Investment and Economic Cooperation until 2008; Cuban

Ambassador in France in 2009; and Cuban Ambassador in Saudi Arabia in 2017.

Another Cuban student of Arabic in Syria called Armando Vergara Bueno, sent by the Foreign Trade Ministry, held the position of General Secretary of the Communist Youth League in the Cuban Embassy. In November 2007, Vergara was accredited as Cuban Ambassador in Qatar. I suppose his appointment must have been influenced by his personal relations with his classmate in the Arabic courses in Syria, Orlando Requeijo, who was already Deputy Minister of Cuban Foreign Affairs that year and had been previously Ambassador to that same country.

CHAPTER V

ARMS TRAFFICKING

1981

In one of those rare nights when we had no diplomatic events and were home leading a family life, Mirita and I were watching TV. We could pick up Jordanian TV programming, where they aired U.S. famous series such as *Dallas, Dynasty, The A Team, The Fantastic Car, The Bionic Woman,* and several musicals.

With the kids already in bed, I told Mirita:

"Early morning tomorrow, I have to drive to Lebanon, but I hope to get back by nighttime. Any situation you may have or if you need any help, you can call Barreiro (the Military Attaché), who will help you".

"Alright", Mirita said, "please, take care and don't do crazy things. Let me know how it went when you get back to Damascus".

Out of discipline, following the compartmentalization principle, according to which we must know and have access only to what pertains to us, and not out of mistrust, I did not give Mirita details of what the specific mission was for me to go to Lebanon, although she knew it was related to the Palestinians affairs.

Lt. Col. Miguel Barreiro had replaced the previous military attaché, Maj. Jose Hernandez Soto. But Barreiro not only represented the Ministry of the Armed Forces (, but he was also an official from the Military Intelligence Division (DIM). He and I began a greater cooperation on information interchange and other tasks, but we sent our reports and carried out operations independently,

The undercover operations I was involved in, as a Foreign Ministry official, were basically to procure and send Western-made weapons to Cuba. I had no idea what their destination was at that time, but later I found out they were to be shipped to Latin America. This had to do with the Special Operations General Division of the Interior Ministry and not by the Army Forces; that was why the military attaché was not involved.

At 7 a.m. the next day, I put four empty diplomatic bags in my car trunk, checked my pistol and played instrumental music by Frank Purcell, one of my favorites, to chill out while driving.

I left for the Syrian border towards Lebanon. The route was amusing because it passed through mountains, cliffs, and dangerous, winding, and narrow roads. On arriving, I got out of the car and showed my passport and diplomatic ID to go through the formalities at customs, but they told me that as a diplomat accredited in Syria, and especially coming from a friendly country like Cuba, I could drive with the diplomatic plates through a military passageway by the side of the customs area.

I was traveling with the intent of meeting one of the members of the Politburo of one of the Palestinian Fronts: the head of the military section, who, by our request, would personally hand me over some weapons in one of their bases in the Lebanese Bekaa, near the city of Chtaura.

After leaving the Syrian border, I crossed a desolate piece of land about two miles long, known as "nobody's land", a stretch that separates the Syrian and Lebanese borders. When I reached the Lebanese border, I had to go through customs paperwork, which was easy for a person with diplomatic passport and plates. Thereafter, I would make this trip at least twenty-five times more during my seven-year stay in Syria.

Once I pass the Lebanese border, I hit the first city, Chtaura, which was full of life with markets and shops of all kinds with good prices. There I went to the Habibi Café, where waiting for me was a guerrilla fighter. As soon as he saw my car, which I had recently traded for a new Mazda model, with, of course, Syrian diplomatic plates, he went out to welcome me. The young Palestinian was wearing jeans, a military cap, a Palestinian scarf, and a moustache. He addressed me in Arabic:

"Marhaba", my name is Abu Youssef, Comrade Saleh sent me to welcome you".

"Salah Malecum" Abu Youssef, my name is Hector. I'm sorry, but I know only a few words in Arabic", I answered.

"Sadik (friend), you look like an Arab", he said.

"Don't worry, I'm Cuban", we both smiled.

It was not the first time since I arrived in the Middle East that I was addressed in Arabic thinking I was an Arab, sometimes even insisting and smiling believing I was kidding. My looks were similar to theirs and that was precisely I had been assigned to work in that region.

French is spoken in several Arab countries like Syria, Lebanon, Morocco, Algeria, and Tunisia for being former French colonies, but most of the Palestinians, Iraqis, Egyptians, and Jordanians speak English for having been colonized by the British, except for some people who studied in France, and, therefore, also spoke French.

"Where is Comrade Saleh?, I asked him.

"First, let me invite you to tea or coffee", the Palestinian responded.

I ordered an espresso coffee. He had Arab-style coffee (Kahwa), which is served very black and sour in a very small cup. Some have Turkish coffee (Kahvesi), which they drank after its sludge settled at the bottom of the cup.

After an almost non-existent conversation, the young Palestinian asked me to go with him in a Mercedes Benz. But I would rather follow him in my own car, since that was one of the basic principles I adhered to keep me moving freely.

We drove down a winding narrow two-way road in a sparsely populated rural area. In about twenty minutes, we entered an old mansion with columns and large lounges, from where several men with guns emerged immediately. I got out of the car and was led to a room where the member of the Politburo of the Democratic Front for the Liberation of Palestine (FDLP in Spanish), Saleh, was sitting behind a large desk.

"Ahla wa sahla" (welcome), Comrade Aguililla".

"Marhaba (Hi), Saleh", I replied shaking hands.

"How are Comrades Fidel, Raul, Ramiro, Abrahantes, and Patricio?", he asked naming one by one.

The Palestinian leader was referring to the Revolution Commander Ramiro Valdes, Politburo member; General Jose Abrahantes, then Interior Minister, and General Patricio de la Guardia, Deputy Minister of the Interior and head of Special Troops Operations back then.

By the way, General Abrahantes was sentenced to twenty years behind bars in 1989 in lawsuits 1 and 2, in which Division General Arnaldo Ochoa was also sentenced to death by firing squad for trafficking diamonds and ivory in Africa. Abrahantes died in prison in January 1991. Rumor has it that he was murdered. General Patricio de la Guardia was given a thirty-year sentence. He bought U.S. weapons seized in Vietnam for the Colombian drug cartels. His twin brother, Colonel Tony de la Guardia, who headed the MC Department (Trade Wall) in the Interior Ministry was also sentenced to a firing squad death penalty due to business with the Colombian drug cartels, too. Tony was a sort of a "Cuban James Bond" and carried out intelligence missions, even within U.S. territory under orders by Fidel Castro himself.

"They are all alright, thank you very much", I reacted. "They send you greetings and I was entrusted by Fidel to send his regards to Comrade Nayef Hawatmeh (FDLP General Secretary). I guess you still have memories of Havana", I added.

"Yes, how can I forget? he asserted, "Today we are precisely complying with the agreement during the last (secret) visit to Cuba a year ago. Besides, I'm pleased that Fidel is offering us student scholarship visas and training for a group of our young Palestinians who will go every year to study diverse university majors and be trained in various military facilities", he pointed out.

The Palestinian leader ordered 'Chai' (tea) for us. I found it tasty; it was not an ordinary one. It seems they added some other aromatic herbs that gave it a very special color, smell, and taste. I remembered that if you wanted more tea, you had to hold the cup turning your wrist sideways. If you did not want more, then you had to place your index finger crossing the cup edge as a sign you were pleased and did not want another serving.

Cuba indeed offered a specific number of scholarships yearly not only to that Front, but also to other Palestinian organizations included in the Palestinian Liberation Organization (PLO) led by Yasser Arafat.

Cuba had a greater cooperation with some of these organizations with a Marxist-Leninist leaning, such as the Democratic Front for the Liberation of Palestine and the Popular Front for the Liberation of Palestine. Not only scholarships in Cuba were offered with all expenses paid for studies of Medicine and Engineering in the university, but also for the Communist Party's National School, where they studied Marxism, and for the Special Troops General Division. In the latter, they were trained in several specialties, such as secret writing, encoded messages, sharpshooting, passport forgery, amphibious commandos (known as frog men), and security in general.

"For us, it is a great pleasure to be able to further our Cuban brothers with this weapons request", Saleh the Front military chief concluded.

Next, he gestured, and two men brought a box with weapons, took out some and put them on the desk immediately. Those were special ops weapons, such as smoke-grenade launchers, machine pistols or submachine guns, automatic handguns, infrared rifles, and silencers. They were made in Israel, Belgium, Italy, and the United States. Saleh proceeded to show me one by one explaining how they worked, with a deep and strong voice, typical of a military chief.

"Chukran (thank you) Comrade Saleh, tell them to put them inside the diplomatic bags that are in the trunk, please", I specified.

Immediately afterwards, we entered another room where served on large tables were assorted fruits and typical Arab Palestinian food and dishes such as "Tabule" (a salad made of parsley, mint, wheat, tomato and onion with oil and lemon, chopped in very small pieces); "homos" (cream with chickpea, sesame, garlic, sweet pepper, and olive oil); "BabaGhanush" (a cream similar to homos but made with eggplant); green rice, pilaf rice, and roast lamb, the latter being the main course.

The typical way Palestinians eat rice is by making small scoops with their hands. But there were also dishes with whole fried little birds, kibbeh (a mixture of lean beef, goat, lamb, fish or camel mincemeat, bulgur cracked wheat, chopped onions and several spices, , forming a crispy hollow shell or stuffed croquettes) and slices of cucumber with garlic inside a bowl of soup with Arab yogurt, bread, and sweets.

The interpreter did not eat at all and did not move away from the Palestinian military chief.

"Saleh, I can't help but notice that most of Palestinian names begin with Abu, but not with their names. I'd like to know the reason why".

"In Palestinian tradition, Abu means "father of". If for instance, your son's name is Jose, you'd be called Abu Jose. In my case, I don't have children, that's why I'm simply called Saleh".

Definitively, traditions in that Arab world were strange, but at the same time interesting, I thought.

We finished having lunch, and after listening to descriptions of the reasons why the Palestinian people fought and their showdown against Israel and the United States, I decided to say goodbyes because it was getting dark.

"Commander, I'm very grateful for all your courtesies and your invitation to have lunch, especially for your presence. I must leave for Damascus with the valuable load".

"For us, it's always a pleasure to partake with a Cuban comrade. Please, send my regards to Comrades Fidel, Raul,

Ramiro, Abrahantes, and Patricio. Of course, to the Ambassador, too", Salen responded.

"Absolutely. I'll convey your greetings. "Chukran". I hope we can meet again soon in Damascus. "Marsalami" (goodbye)", I concluded.

Every time I could, I said some words in Arabic, which they logically appreciated with affection.

I was going back with four diplomatic bags full of weapons in the car trunk and had to go across two borders. On the Syrian side, I would be protected by my diplomatic immunity, since that was the country I was accredited in; they would even let me go through the military passageway. But in the Lebanese one, that was not the case, although diplomatic privileges somehow protected me.

At the time, I did not know the real destination of those weapons, but later I found out they would be sent for subversion and violence in some Latin American countries through Cuba.

At that point, I actually acted almost mechanically in order to do my job. I had been trained to comply with instructions without questioning them, abiding by the secret of information.

When I reached the Lebanese border, I parked in a dark place a bit away from the office where I headed to deal with the paperwork; when I got back to the car, I realized I had locked it with the key inside. As I had the weapons in the trunk, I did not hesitate to quicky hit one of the car's windows with the elbow of the arm trying to avoid drawing anybody's attention, but I did not manage to break it. I knew I could hurt myself because I did not protect my arm. Then I tried with the handgun handle and got it broken. A Lebanese guard showed up and asked me in Arabic:

"What's going on here?"

I hid the gun and explained to him in French.

"Mr. Officer, everything is fine. What happened was that I left the key inside the car; that's why I tried to break the window".

In Lebanon, French is more spoken than in Syria.

"Let me see your papers", the officer ordered.

I was aware of the risk the operation was running because the officer was likely to also ask me to open the trunk to check it out. So, I got also mentally ready to neutralize him by force if necessary, taking advantage of the darkness in that area and the fact that the guard had not seen the car plates well yet.

When the guard approached me, I told him:

"Look at my documents, diplomatic passport".

The officer, who was a tall, strong man, got close and, thank God, said:

"Very well, you may go on".

I got in the car and despite the tense moment, I drove at a moderate speed towards the so-called "nobody's land", where I did put the pedal to the metal. When I arrived at the Syrian border, I went through the military passageway non-stop and entered Syrian territory without declaring anything at customs, since I was allowed to do it for being accredited in Syria using diplomatic plates.

I reached Damascus without any more incidents, and after making sure no one was following me, I headed home.

Since the embassy was facing the Presidential Palace, it was not convenient to unload the weapons there. I had double protection in my place for living in the Ambassador's residence penthouse.

I kept some weapons on the closet floor of my bedroom and others in the room I used as an office because it would be just for a few days.

I explained to Mirita that the weapons would be there temporarily, which she understood without objections. After eating a light meal, I went to bed and had a sound sleep.

Some days later, I took Mirita and Maitelis on the road to visit Beirut as it was a very entertaining trip.

When we arrived at the Cuban Embassy in Lebanon, I told an official we had gone down a deserted avenue in the city, and that had given me a bad impression. He replied that such avenue had been blocked by snipers and we had been very lucky not to have been shot at.

On the way back, we took another street, but despite that Mirita told me:

"Look at that smoke coming from your left".

As I looked, I realized it was an anti-aircraft machine gun shooting, but since the radio was on and the windows were up, I had not noticed. That was normal in Beirut.

We took another highway and, a short while later, we came across some tanks and a military check-up point. We asked about the route to get to Damascus and a soldier with bright gold teeth explained to us we were heading toward Israel. The soldier was a Sudanese officer member of the so-called Arab Deterrent Forces.

We finally took the right road and reached Damascus without any further issues.

In Lebanon, there was a large mosaic of military forces. Besides the small Lebanese army and its security forces, present were the Syrian army, mainly in the Bekaa, and the Israeli army in the country's south.

There were also military forces belonging to Palestinian organizations, militias of the so-called Lebanese progressive forces, the Druze, the falangist militias of families such as Gemayel, and other families like Frangieh, and Joumblat. And furthermore, Muslim extremists like Hezbollah, Hamas, and the Islamic Jihad. Some of them were supported by Iran.

Additionally, Lebanon was eventually a haven for terrorists such as Carlos, the Jackal, born in Venezuela in 1949, whose real name was Ilich Ramirez Sanchez. He was convicted in 1997 in France, and former President Hugo Chavez tried to vindicate him by calling him "a revolutionary".

For the reader to have an idea of Carlos the Jackal's links with the Middle East, suffice it to say that he was recruited and nicknamed like that, according to Wikipedia, by the Palestinian terrorist Bassam Abu Sharif, for him to become a member of the People's Front for the Liberation of Palestine in 1970. Abu Sharif was, in turn, called the "face of terror" by the *Time* magazine over his participation that year in the hijacking of flights 741 of TWA, 100 of "Swiss Air", and 219 of "El Al". Later, Sharif became security advisor to Yasser Arafat and was ousted from the Popular Front in 1987. Subsequently, he was appointed presidential advisor in the newly created Palestinian National Authority in 1996.

Lebanon, previously known as "the Middle East Switzerland", was at present devastated by wars and internal fighting, particularly in the city of Beirut.

On a personal level, I like Beirut a lot and it reminded me of Havana for being a city that also has high-rise buildings and a waterside wall on the coast with a view to the sea.

Already back in Damascus, I held a meeting with Abu Nidal, a member of the FPLP's Politburo, and later, accompanying the Ambassador, another meeting with its General Secretary, George Habache. The latter invited us to his home and presented Ambassador Lester Rodriguez with a very light chromed handgun.

Likewise, we were invited to Nayef Hawatmeh's place. He was the FDLP's General Secretary, with whom Cuba had close ties.

Moreover, I had meetings with Abu Leyla, a member of the Politburo's such front, who connected me with the Head of Information of his Front, Mustafa. The latter spoke perfect French, because he studied in Paris. We held numerous talks, and he provided me with profiles of a great number Palestinian leaders. That information, coupled with others we already had, contained a large file on each Palestinian leader from the different Palestinian factions and the PLO. The info was handed over by the Ambassador to the Intelligence General Division (DGI, currently DI).

The wives of Palestinian leaders Abu Leyla and Mustafa, named Teresa and Samanta, respectively, often visited Mirita in our place because they spoke Spanish, since they were Palestinians who were raised in Morocco. One of them had been jailed in Israel.

Melba Hernandez, one of the only two Cuban women taking part in the attack on the Moncada garrison in Cuba together with Fidel Castro in 1953, and former Cuban Ambassador in Vietnam and Cambodia, visited Damascus.

The Palestinian Women's Federation held a ceremony in her honor. Mirita attended this political event with our little daughter Maitelis (who was about 4 years old). During the event, Maitelis told Nihaya, an Embassy's Palestinian interpreter, that she wanted to take the floor and deliver a speech during the event. Mirita nodded smiling, so Maitelis stood before the Palestinian audience stage fright free and delivered a short "Speech" translated by Nihaya.

Without really knowing the meaning of what she said, and with a lot of inconsistencies due to her short age, Maitelis said, among other things:

"Imperialism has to be locked in a pit. Imperialism is bad. I am a Cuban girl. Palestinians are my friends".

About nine hundred Palestinians present laughed and applauded her words.

Samanta, Mustafa's wife, presented Maitelis with a small gold replica of the map of Palestine for her to put it in her necklace, and said that when Maitelis grew up, she could command "a battalion of male soldiers".

In October 1983, the United States launched operation 'Urgent Fury' together with other nations from the Eastern Caribbean Organization of States, to invade the island of Grenada. When Cuba learned of the invasion, it sent Colonel Pedro Tortoló to organize a resistance with about seven hundred eighty troops, mainly military engineers and construction workers, who helped to build a new airport, as well as some eighteen hundred Grenadians.

The Cuban Embassy in Damascus received a message from Havana stating that "there was a group of Cubans hugging the flag and resisting the U.S. invasion in Grenada", and I was told I had to publicize solidarity and support messages.

I called on the Syrian government, the Bass Party, the PLO, several Palestinian organizations, the Syrian Communist Party and other Syrian political and mass organizations, as well as other representations in the area. I traveled around Damascus requesting messages of solidarity and support.

My actions had good results because several messages were published. But two days later, we found out that Colonel Tortoló, a Cuban armed forces officer sent to organize resistance, had quickly taken refuge in the Russian Embassy in Grenada. In Cuba, some people mocked him with the following: "If you want to run fast, buy Tortoló tennis shoes". Colonel Tortoló was court-martialed, degraded, and sentenced to join the Cuban troops fighting in Angola.

Despite that individual's attitude, from what I have read in several articles, the battle lasted several days, notwithstanding the U.S. forces' superiority in troops, navy, and air, including attack helicopters and naval artillery.

That same year, in a November 1983 night in Syria, while Mirita and I were in the penthouse where we lived, loud shots and explosions were heard together with shootouts of diverse calibers and weapons; we could see the tracer bullets flying in the sky. I went out to the balcony to try to figure out what was going on, and I felt a bullet pass very close to me. Then I started calling all the Embassy native employees to see whether they knew what was happening. They told me that the Syrian TV was reporting President Hafez El Assad's discharge from the hospital where he had been admitted for several days due to a heart attack. The shots had been made from joy thanks to the President's recovery.

During the President's sickness, his brother Rifat El Assad tried to stage a coup d'etat,

We had limited movement in the embassy because of the increased security around the Presidential Palace, which was right across the street. For a couple of days, we were not allowed to park our cars in front of the embassy and the guards were pointing their guns in alert position all the time.

I had to park far from the embassy, and when I was walking towards it, the guards blocked my pace. Since they did not accept any explanation, I argued with one guard who then pointed his gun at me, yielding his AK-47 with the bayonet out, but an official ordered him to let me go through to the Palace offices. There I could speak with the head of protocol of the president, who allowed us to have more flexible means to get in and out of our embassy, which was practically blockaded.

As a result of the coup d'etat attempt, the President stripped his brother Rifat of the military forces under his command, which were around 55,000 troops equipped with tanks, artillery, and helicopters, and named him to be just like one of the three existing vice presidents aimed at diminishing his royal powers.

However, two months after my departure from Syria, in May 1984, during a health relapse of the President, his brother Rifat tried a new coup d'etat again.

This time Rifat was sent abroad for alleged "diplomatic tours" and, finally, was threatened with death if he ever returned to Syria. Rifat was a multimillionaire and alternated his stays in luxurious homes in Marbella, Geneva, Paris, and London.

When his brother Hafez died on June 10th, 2000, Rifat considered himself the national heir to the Syrian Presidency and challenged Bashar, son of Hafez. But no one endorsed the former, so he could not return and stayed in exile, all forgotten. Rifat is regarded as a criminal in Syria because he committed too many crimes of abuse and corruption to enrich himself.

CHAPTER VI

UNDERCOVER OPERATIONS

INTENSIFY

1982

I kept the weapons, I had brought from Lebanon hidden in my penthouse waiting for the diplomatic couriers. The day they arrived I drove to the new Damascus International Airport that had been operated for just a few years ago.

The then relatively new airport building was large and sumptuous. It had a separate room for those who would want to pray. There was also a protocol hall for diplomats, leaders, and top personalities. You no longer saw either beggars or people praying in the hallways or the crowd chanting like when I first arrived in the country. At present, this airport is about forty-five years old and has become inadequate due to the increase of over fifty percent of passengers and flights; that is why the Syrian Transportation Minister, Mr. Ali Hamoud, declared in 2017 that there is a project for a new international airport to be built in Damascus. It seems that internal problems and clashes have delayed it.

The diplomatic couriers arrived from Prague. On this occasion, they were two special agents from the General intelligence Division (DGI) who had been specifically assigned for this operation. Both were well stout, and one of them was paradoxically called "Tiny" when he was actually about 7.4 feet tall. These couriers would bring the weapons in diplomatic bags which, under the Vienna Convention, could not be opened or inspected at airports. Both were trained to make bags look light in weight although they carried heavy stuff.

I invited these couriers to dine at my place. I had already been warned about Tiny's voracious appetite, so I did not want to miss the show. There were anecdotes about how he had killed an attacking dog with just a punch; in Mexico, he ate tacos ten at a time, etc. We served him a big bowl with six big beef steaks plus rice, black beans, yucca, and vegetable salad. The rest of us ate the regular size.

Tiny devoured the six steaks like eating crackers. He told us that the Interior Ministry gave him and his family an extra special quota of food, since he had two children who were also huge.

The specially selected weapons were taken to Cuba through the diplomatic couriers, from where they would be delivered to guerrilla fighters in El Salvador, Guatemala, Chile, and other Latin American countries. Of course, at that time I did not know the weapons destination. That was top-secret information.

The Castros' government has always carried out subversive operations with intelligence and military support goals intended for communist and antidemocratic movements in almost all over the globe in order to try to export communism, not only in Latin America and the Caribbean, but also in Africa, the Middle East, and even Europe.

At first, there were small amounts of special weapons for guerrilla fighters in Latin America to carry through bank robberies, kidnappings, hostage takings, and murders (something I learned about much later). Those weapon-trafficking operations were held and increased with time.

There were different suppliers available in the Middle East during my mission (until 1984) and nearly two years afterwards. Some of the weapons also fell in drug caftel hands, such as U.S. weapons the Vietnamese had stored and sold to drug dealers.

I occasionally visited some Palestinian camps, where I practice shooting and watched their military training.

Once I set up a hand-to-hand combat exhibition by Palestinians for all the embassy staff and their relatives. The Palestinians showed how to make and operate explosive with materials available in pharmacies; simulated infiltration through barricade replicas used in Israeli borders; did target shooting; and finally, a typical Palestinian lunch was served.

The Palestinian Liberation Organization (PLO) had an executive committee whose chairman was Yasser Arafat. Besides, there was a national council, which was like a parliament in exile. The latter brought together several

Palestinian organizations representing different trends such as:

- Al Fatah: a majority right-wing organization with a broad membership, with the PLO Chairman Yasser Arafat as its leader.
- The Democratic Front for the Liberation of Palestine (FDLP) with a Marxist ideology, the general secretary of which was Nayef Hawatmeh.
- The Popular Front for the Liberation of Palestine (PFLP)
- Also with a Marxist ideology, but more radical, led by George Habache.
- Al Saika: an organization sponsored by Syria
- The Popular Front for the Liberation of Palestine-General Command, also pro-Syrian, led by Ahmad Jibril.
- The Arab Liberation Front, linked to the Bass Party.
- And other terrorist groups like Abu Abas and Abu Nidal, which had support by and hideouts in countries such as Lybia, Syria, and Iraq.

The PLO had diplomatic representations in some countries and bodies such as Cuba, Spain, France, the UN, etc. It was provided with financial aid from many Arab countries, including Saudi Arabia.

In one of the visits by the then Cuban Foreign Minister, Isidoro Malmierca Peoli, when I was Charge D'Affairs, a.i., I arranged a meeting with Yasser Arafat. A Palestinian member of the latter's bodyguards led us to a secret place for the meeting, where, for two hours, we listened to Arafat, who displayed a map on the wall during his speech. I remember, I was taking down notes with a ballpoint pen, as usual, when the sound of the pen click called Arafat's attention, who stopped speaking and stared at me. His face looked like that of a rat.

PLO President Yasser Arafat:

When Yasser Arafat died on November 11th, 2004, he had hundreds of millions of dollars stolen from the Palestinian people's cause: money that had been donated by diverse Arab countries and other parts of the world as aid to the PLO for many years. A long litigation ensued between his widow and the Palestinian authorities over the secret Arafat's bank accounts. She kept the private plane, part of the wealth, and a millionaire pension.

Our Ambassador was accompanied by me to frequent meetings with several members of the PLO's Executive

Committee, such as Farouk Khadumi, head of the International Relations Department, a kind of PLO's Foreign Minister, and Mahmud Abbas, known as Abu Mazzen, spokesman of the PLO's Executive Committee, who became President of the Palestinian National Authority, in January 2005 after Arafat's death.

The Palestinian National Authority (PNA) is an autonomous administrative organization which governs parts of Cisjordania and the Gaza Strip since 1994. It came into being that year by the Oslo Accords between the PLO and the Israeli government. Yasser Arafat was their first Chairman and remained in charge until his death in 2004.

Parallel to the activities and contacts with most of the Palestinian Organization leaders, I did my diplomatic work by organizing cultural exhibitions, close-circle cocktail parties, attending receptions, and having meetings with Syrian authorities. Another most important steady source of information we had was a monthly confidential contact held with a representative of the Syrian Communist Party, planned by its General Secretary, Khaled Bagdache. This contact, called, Kartouche, kept us up to date on the Syrian inner issues. He met with the Ambassador or with me, according to the circumstances and timing.

The Syrian Communist Party was official and represented by two ministers in the Cabinet. Its General Secretary, Khaled Bagdache, was considered a historic personality because he founded the first Communist Parties of Syria and Lebanon in 1927.

Damascus, Syria, 1980. Left to right: Author, Mr. Hector G. Aguililla, Cuban Charge D' Affairs a.i.; Mr. Khale Bagdache, General Secretary of the Syrian Communist Party; Mrs. Bagdache; and Mrs. Miriam Aguililla.

I had another contact with an underground representative of the Jordanian Communist Party in Syria, which was deemed an illegal party in his country, which also bordered Syria. When I restarted contacts with him, I followed the procedure set by my predecessor: I went to a Mercedes Benz spare part shop in the city's downtown area and stood facing one of its showcase windows. There I could see the sales assistants, fixed my tie as a sign and kept walking slowly. A man came out right away, approached me and said in Spanish:

-"Get in your car and follow that white Mercedes Benz you see over there".

After driving for a few minutes and checking no one followed us, the man parked in a plaza and hopped in my car telling me:

"Salam Malecum", (Hi, peace be with you)

"Malecum Salam", (peace be with you, too), I answered.

"My name is Ali", he added. "Cuban comrades have not contacted me in the last two months. We used to have monthly meetings".

"Comrade Ali," I said, "I would have liked to contact you before, but I got here in Damascus recently, and I've been really busy catching up with everything. We are very much interested in continuing contacts with you, since the Cuban Communist Party wants to logically strenghten relations with your party. I suggest we agree on a new sign and the dates we'll meet from now on to exchange ideas, with more time and safety. For that purpose, we could meet this Friday at 7 pm at the Norah market".

"Yes, perfect. I'd like to take the opportunity to take you to my place to have dinner, and then we'll go along with all that. I'd like you to bring your wife and, if you have children, too. I want you to meet my family and taste the typical Jordanian food", he added.

"Agreed", I responded, "it'll be a pleasure. See you there. Now, please, you'd rather leave first."

I liked the invitation because I could also bring my family. Besides, the representative of the Jordanian Communist Party was a very important steady information source for my work. He was under covert status in Damascus because his party was illegal in the Jordanian monarchy. His presence could damage the relations between Syria and that country, but the Syrians looked away as long as he remained clandestine and the Jordanians were not aware of his dealings.

The food was delicious, with a variety of plates from Jordan. His wife behaved like a progressive woman by dressing and sharing with us like we do in the West. We had wine and arac, the latter being a typical Arab drink similar to anise.

This representative of the Jordanian Communist Party this time gave me a summary of the major events and info he had on the internal affairs in Jordan and the regional conflict. Later on, I drew up a special report for Havana addressed to the Foreign Relations Department of the PCC's Central Committee and the Foreign Ministry's North Africa and the Middle East Division.

Before long, we received a coded cable by Jose Abrahantes, then Interior Minister, who asked us to fully cooperate with an official from the Special Operations Division, who was coming to carry out a secret mission.

145

At the airport, I welcomed Major Florentino Rodriguez, who told me, that, besides his military career, he had studied law. He was coming from Prague, Czechoslovakia, and on the way to the embassy, he told me:

"Aguililla, I need you to help me ASAP to find me a contact with the Syrian authorities that can make it easy to transport and authorize the transfer of a large weapons cargo from Lebanon to a Syrian port. This is a very secret operation. Once, the Mossad (Israel's intelligence) found out about the transfer of a similar cargo in a Cuban ship and sank it. In the embassy, only you and the Ambassador must know it, no one else, not even the military attaché. You can say I'm a representative of the Culture or Foreign Trade Ministry, as you deem best".

"Very well, Florentino." I answered. "I have very good relations with the Bass Party's Foreign Relations Department, which is the ruling party here, and tomorrow I'll request a meeting. In my opinion, due to the history of cooperation in our bilateral relations, and the Syrian foreign policy, they will not deny their support".

"Good. It depends on you to have the ideal readiness to carry out this operation", Major Florentino replied.

The next day, I requested a meeting with Mr. Charif, an official of the Bass Party's Foreign Relations Department, who was generally in charge of relations with Cuba, and told me they would speak with the head of a military unit in

Damascus so we could get all the necessary support. They never told me which unit it was but I guessed it was a military unit belonging to the Syrian Special Forces commanded by General Ali Haydar.

Florentino joined me in that meeting, arranged by the Bass Party with the head of the Syrian military unit, where everything was laid out. The Syrian official promised to give us all the military trucks, between eight and ten, to move the weapons that would go through the Lebanese and Syrian borders and cross the Syrian territory all the way to the port of destination in the Syrian Mediterranean coast. The cargo would be unloaded in a Cuban ship that carried sugar from Cuba to Syria.

Part of this big shipment of Western-made weapons was financed by Cuba. The former official of the General Intelligence Division, Major Manuel De Beunza, who worked for the State Council's Department 4, in charge of finances and personal wealth of Fidel Castro, confirmed in his first TV interview in a Miami Hispanic channel in November 2009, that he personally had taken "a steel briefcase full of US dollars to Beirut for the Arafat's Palestinians". It is likely that that money was earmarked for buying new weapons for latin american guerrillas because Arafat actually did not need any financial aid. Just like Fidel, Mr. Arafat was a multimillionaire. We rather had info on Arafat who, eventually, was lending money to some nations, including Cuba.

Another big chunk of the weapons was donations made by the Arab Democratic Republic of Yemen, the Communist Party of several Arab countries, and the Palestinians themselves.

It was rather impressive to see how Cuba, so small, developed so much activity and was the operational center, supported by the Soviet Union, of international conspiracy and subversion against democracy, especially against the U.S. policies and interests all over the world.

I accompanied Major Florentino to another meeting with a Palestinian organization which he asked for an ammo cargo which would be sent via Prague or Berlin to Cuba.

In reality, not even myself knew all the details in this case of its transportation but I did hear they mentioned, among the supply sources, the Italian mafia.

In such meeting, the head of the Palestinian Front security called me aside and told me confidentially:

"The day after tomorrow at 7 am, we are going to sink one of the U.S. military ships off the Beirut coast".

" How are you going to do it?" I indiscreetly asked on purpose.

"Our amphibious men, trained in Cuba, will place explosives, and this will be a warning to the U.S. to stop supporting Israel, and put pressure on the PLO and the Arab countries to accept the imposed conditions for mediated solutions in the conflict. We'll only accept peace through the unconditional creation of a free independent Palestinian state and the withdrawal of Israel from the occupied Arab territories."

"I hope there won't be civilian casualties in this operation" I chimed in.

The head of the Palestinian Front security answered:

"Comrade Aguililla, the United States is an accomplice of Israel, which kills our sons, and brothers on a daily basis, and nobody cares about it. This is about the military bombing and trying to massacre our Palestinian people and intimidate the Arab world. When in the West they learn of the death of two or three Christians or Jews, they make it widely known condemning it on TV and the press. They raise hell about it, but when tens of our Palestinians and Muslim brothers are killed, they don't care.

"I understand. We'll meet again soon". Shrukan, Marsalami", I thanked him and took my leave.

I really left to avoid major disagreements with this Palestinian leader, since I was not going to solve anything at all and would mar my working relations, but I wished I would let the Americans know of the operation to avoid casualties. For this reason, I decided to tell Carlos, the Panamanian Charge D'Affairs linked to the CIA, a rather incomplete version of it I knew he would take care of using his imagination to bring the idea together.

Indeed, while already in the United States, I could confirm through a CIA officer, that Carlos had reported at that time that Palestinians, with the participation of an alleged plane transmitting radio codes screaming through a megaphone "Mayday, Mayday, Mayday", would simulate it was falling down, and would attack the ship. Somehow, the Americans, by reinforcing the ship security (including their own amphibious men who guarded the vessel), thwarted the operation attempt by the extremist Palestinians who failed in their venture.

The day came when Syrian military trucks transported the weapons stored in the Lebanese Beqaa to the Syrian port of Latakia in the Mediterranean. There, a Cuban ship supposedly carrying sugar, sailed off will all the cargo. These Western-made weapons had been partially bought by the Cuban government and in part donated by the Yemen's People's Democratic Republic, the region's communist parties, and the major Palestinian organizations.

On another occasion, when I had to go to the Latakia port to see to a Cuban ship, the military attaché, Lieutenant Colonel Miguel Barreiro, volunteered to join me. On the way there, Barreiro's car broke down and I called Mirita on the phone and told her:

"Barreiro's car broke down when running over "a lying police officer" that he could not see in time. We'll have to have the car towed to get back".

When we returned to Damascus, we learned that Mirita and Barreiro's wife, Teresa, had been scared to death because they thought that Barreiro had run over a Syrian police officer. What they did not know was that a speed bump was called in Cuba " a lying police officer ".

Shortly before this trip, Lieutenant Colonel Barreiro had hit a Palestinian girl with a diplomatic-plated car and the girl had been injured. Someone at the scene punched Barreiro in the mouth, and the police apprehended him. He called me to let me know about it because I was the Charge D'Affairs, a.i. I hastily reached the head of the Syrian Defense Ministry's Protocol Division, who interceded in the case and later informed me to personally go and get the Lieutenant Colonel released.

When I arrived at the police station, Barreiro was handcuffed and sitting on a bench next to other detainees. As soon as I ID'd myself, he was released and we headed to our homes. Later on, under my suggestion, Barreiro visited the girl in the hospital with a bouquet of flowers.

During my daily work, I had to accompany visiting official delegations of high-ranking Cuban leaders to Syria many times to meetings on bilateral relations matters, conflict mediations, how to get votes in international bodies, or to bring personal invitations from Fidel Castro because, at that time, Cuba was presiding over the Non-Aligned Countries Movement. Thus, I had the opportunity to meet high-ranking

Arabs and Palestinians; among them, the heads of state from Syria, Lybia, Democratic Yemen, and the heads of Palestinian organizations, including Yasser Arafat.

On occasions, I had to wait at the Syrian-Iraqi border for the Cuban Foreign Minister, Isidoro Malmierca, to drive him down the highway to Damascus and Lebanon and vice versa, since he frequently traveled in the region to mediate in the Iraq-Iran conflict.

Likewise, sometimes I welcomed Minister Malmierca at the Damascus airport because, on such endeavors, he sometimes, flew international airlines, and, other times, on a Fidel's Cuban plane. It was only logical that when flying the Cuban plane, landing permit, stay, take off, flight route, and crew hotels, etc., had to be arranged and paid.

Iraq had a particular circumstance in its bilateral relations with Cuba due to the fact that President Saddam Hussein suffered from an ulcer in the spine. He had seen several specialists from different countries, but only the Cuban orthopedist, Dr. Rodrigo Alvarez Cambra, found a cure. Such a disease had prevented Saddam Hussein from having sex relations and walking properly. Due to the Arab machismo, his limitations were far graver for him.

Saddam Hussein requested to see Dr. Alvarez Cambra frequently; he would send his personal airplane for the latter to go to Iraq from Cuba. The doctor turned up to have such access and personal relationship with Saddam that, on

152

many occasions, when a major topic had to be discussed with the President, it was not the Cuban Ambassador in Bagdhad who met him but Dr. Rodrigo Alvarez Cambra himself as a special envoy sent by Fidel.

Saddam presented the doctor with an air-conditioned house in Havana and a Mercedes Benz car, according with comments from cuban diplomatic collegues in Bagdad, who also said that when he flew back to Cuba and made a stopover in Paris, Saddam would give him $10,000 US dollars as "out-of-pocket" expenses, and was welcomed at the airport by the Iraqi Ambassador.

In addition, Saddam gave as a gift every official working in the Cuban embassy in Iraq a cooler freezer.

Also I remember at the beginning of 1979, I accompanied the member of the Politburo and Commander of the Revolution, Guillermo Garcia Frias, on the road to the Syrian border with Jordan. This Cuban high-ranking leader traveled to Amman to hand over a personal invitation by Fidel Castro to Jordan's King Hussein for him to attend the Sixth Summit of the Non-Aligned Countries Movement, which would take place in Havana from September 3rd throrugh the 9th.

King Hussein attended the Sixth Summit and presented each Cuban official, who assisted the Jordanian delegation with a solid gold watch with the crown engraved in the back.

When Christmas time got closer, just like every year during this time, my family and I traveled on vacation to Cuba. On the way to Cuba we almost always visited Rome, adorned with beautiful Christmas decorations. We flew via Berlin of the communist Germany just twice, where communication was hard because people spoke German only. In the German restaurants, we looked in the menus for some foods ending in something similar to steak, and it worked for us.

In one of the many flights we took on our way through Rome, the airline Alitalia lodged us in the Sheraton Hotel "Parco Di Medici" due to the flight connection to Madrid. There we chose a room for ourselves and another one adjacent to ours for the two kids. At 2 am, I had a call from the hotel front desk, and I answered the phone. I was spoken to in Italian and the only thing I could understand was "perturbazioni, perturbazioni". I looked out the window, and as it was raining very hard I looked at Mirita, who was also up, and told her:

"I got a call from the hotel front desk, and the only thing I inferred was, allegedly, that there is a cyclone disturbance. It's raining heavily, it seems there's a storm. Maybe they're warning us because we'll probably have to change tomorrow's flight tickets".

"Well, we'll see when it dawns, you'd better go to bed", Mirita, answered.

Five minutes later, I got another call repeating the same thing: "perturbazioni, perturbazioni", but this time I asked the one on the other end if he spoke French. Then he explained to me in French that other guests had complained about noise coming from our children's room and they were bothered by the TV high volume. From there, the word "Perturbazioni" referred to the ones disturbing, ha, ha, ha; we still laugh when we remember that incident due to the funny confusion.

In Madrid, as usual, we had a great time and took the opportunity to buy some personal items and presents for our relatives in Cuba, including medications.

Already in Havana, we would meet our relatives, had the joy to be together on New Year's eve, and enjoy our island's beautiful landscape.

Following tradition, we always went to the countryside and got ourselves a pig that we would roast on December 31st in a rustic grill or a makeshift oven in the backyard.

I rented a car from the existing Special Service back then only for government high-ranking officials and tourists during all our vacation. For that purpose, I had to show an authorized document from the ministry, which was a privilege at the time.

Every year, we rented a cabana for a week in Varadero Beach. On occasions, we took my niece Yokiana with us, who often got seasick during the trip.

We eventually invited my sisters, Isis and Anita, my brothers-in-law, Ramon and Frank, and my now late parents, Hector and Yoky, R.I.P., to that place and others.

Varadero is undoubtedly a paradisiacal place to chill out and enjoy with relatives the natural beauty and quality of one of the best beaches in the world.

Tourists and guests with hard currency were given priority to be lodged in the main hotels and cabanas. Ordinary Cubans had limitations, not only in the famous Varadero Beach, but also in hotels in Havana and all over the country. There came a time when Cubans were forbidden to enter most of the nice places in their own homeland, especially hotels, restaurants, and certain tourist cays and beaches. I remember once I tried to have dinner at the *1830 Restaurant* in Vedado, Havana, and I was rejected over my Cuban citizenship, even having hard currency and being a government official. The country's reality was more depressing every day, and it really hurt and affected the population tremendously.

Fidel Castro pretended to develop a foreign policy, as if it were a Napoleonic power whereas the people were starving and needy. This was due to his excessive ambition for power and fame, and his wicked dementia.

Going back to the topic of our vacation in Cuba, it is worthy to mention that, at the end of the first vacation we enjoyed during Christmas in 1977, I returned to Syria by myself, since, against my will and with regret, Mirita and Maitelis had to stay in Cuba because the former was due in two months to have our new son Hector Eduardo, whom we would affectionally call Eddy.

Back in Syria already, one day I received a happy telex with the news that my son Eddy had been born, and I jumped with joy, since we now had the longed for couple and were a bigger family of four members. That night, I celebrated my son's birth with some members of the mission with whisky and Cuban cigars.

The baby was only forty-five days old when Mirita dared to take that long flight with him and Maitelis alone. When they arrived in Damascus, I welcomed them by the runway in front of the airplane door with a big bouquet of flowers and happiness showing in my face for seeing my family grow safe and sound. Of course, Mirita did not work for some months and devoted her beautiful and necessary duties as mother and wife.

Over time, I became aware more and more of the increasing corruption of the Cuban highest-ranking leaders through my contacts when they sometimes visited Syria. Just to mention a couple of examples, some asked me to have money illegally exchanged in the black market for personal benefit; they bought luxury items such as white Drill 100 suits that former President Batista used to wear, which they criticized so much; they used money from the financial donations to the Cuban mass organizations to buy personal stuff. Besides, they left us a list of items to be bought so that we sent or took them personally when visiting Cuba. These high-ranking leaders were leading a millionaire's life while our people starved. They demagogically claimed there was no social class difference in a socialist society and that we were all the same, when they actually led the population to mysery so they could enrich themselves and live with great privilege.

The socioeconomic development they promised the Cuban people had turned into a fantasy, and every day, the country was left more impoverished and backward, which killed the Cuban youth's dreams and future.

On another matter, as part of my extensive and diverse duties, I helped to establish contacts in Damascus between underground delegations of high-ranking leaders of many organizations, and, in some instances, even with the Syrian Bass party itself. This collaboration among them was not only a political one but also a military assistance and material-wise one, prromoted and sponsored by Cuba.

Fidel Castro shared Che Guevara's theory that "we had to create two, three, many Vietnams", that is, incite conflicts to distract, divide, and weaken "the American imperialism forces".

Other warfare theories by Fidel, which I got to know through officials close to him, were that Cuba was a small country, but it had to be respected just like a great power, and in order to achieve it, if he had to trigger a world nuclear war or blow the United Nations Organization's building into pieces, he was willing to do it. This is a reflection of a personality with an obsessive desire of grandeur and power that reached psycopathic and diabolic extremes.

According to comments by Ambassador Lester Rodriguez, when the so-called "October Crisis" or "Missile Crisis" took place in 1962, Fidel had sent twin brothers, Patricio and Tony De La Guardia, special ops officers, to accompany then Foreign Minister, Raul Roa, to the UN building with two portfolios full of explosives ready to blow the place up if "the invasion" to Cuba was carried out.

1962. Russian missiles deployed in Cuba.

The Threat of Cuban Missiles, 1962

Ambassador Lester also told me that Fidel Castro himself was who pushed the button that took down the well-known US U2 spy plane, an action which almost brought about war.

Likewise, on February 1996, Fidel irresponsibly ordered to shoot down two harmless, small civilian planes from the "Brothers to the Rescue" organization in international waters, which killed four civilians, among them, three US citizens.

Fidel was actually never interested in improving relations with the United States because that permanent conflict was his best pretext to deceive and exacerbate a patriotic feeling in the population facing an alleged foreign invasion. He had everything cold-bloodedly calculated. Besides, he had more ways and means to violate the limited US economic embargo.

During our stay in Damascus, my children Eddy and Maitelis grew up very actively. I sometimes found Eddy, at 3, climbing a fence or a tree in front of the embassy, speaking to a security guard of the presidential palace, who listened as if he understood and amused him. Other times, Eddy got into meetings the Ambassador was holding, and the latter let him stay there.

Sometimes, we found the Ambassador sitting on his office floor playing with Eddy with a ball or a toy truck. When all the staff got together to watch movies in the ambassador's residence, no one dared to tell the Ambassador whether the movie was bad. Then we used Eddy, who would tell him:

"Ambassador, that's a bad movie".

We would look at each other and laughed. Lester paid attention and changed the movie for the delight of all present.

Once, Mirita, in despair. Let me know that Eddy had red spots all over the body. We finally found out that Eddy had placed a chair next to the fridge, climbed up and grabbed a med bottle for allergies called Benadryl. As it had a sweet flavor, he downed it all. We immediately took him to a French hospital in the city. It was late at night, and a nun told me that the doctor was not in, and she could not do anything at all. Upset and helpless, and knowing that my son was intoxicated, I senselessly shouted back at her in a foul manner on my way back to the car:

"That's why you need a revolution in France".

And the nurse shot back:

"I'm more communist than you are".

I realized I had said something absurd.

We usually used the Soviet embassy medical services, but at that late time in the night, I finally decided to take him to a Syrian public hospital. I knew its location and parked in the emergency area.

I helped to hold Eddy, who was strong and had turned restless, while they performed a stomach pumping to detox him. Coincidentally, the Syrian doctor who assisted him had studied in Cuba, spoke Spanish, and was very polite and competent. We got back home with Eddy, who returned to normal very fast. We were not charged at all for the hospital services.

There was another Syrian doctor, who studied in Cuba and married a young Cuban woman, who went to live in Syria. She told us that when her husband was studying in Cuba, they would often go dancing and stayed in the best hotels. And since she arrived in Syria, she was locked in the house under the surveillance of the husband's whole family.

Once, a Cuban musical group came to Damascus, and we arranged a performance in a Syrian theater. We invited the diplomatic corps, Syrian authorities, friends, and Cubans residing in Syria. The young Cuban woman married to the Syrian doctor attended the show together with him, but there was a moment when she could not resist the Cuban contagious rhythm of Cuban music and started dancing. The next day, she arrived at the embassy with bruises in the face and black eyes due to the beating by her husband. She asked crying for help to get away and return to Cuba. We requested authorization and were told to give her an entry permit to Cuba, but she had to pay for her air ticket. Somehow, she managed to raise money to at least pay for a ticket from Damascus to Madrid. She achieved to get away from her Syrian husband, and we took her from the embassy to the airport.

There was also another case of a Cuban woman whose husband died in combat in the Syrian city of Hama against the opposition. When he died, she was inherited by her brother-in-law and arrived in the embassy covered with a black chador pleading for help to escape and return to Cuba. We did the same operation: when she succeeded in paying for the air ticket and reached the embassy, we took her to the airport.

There was another Cuban woman in Jordan who reached to us by phone for being also a victim of her Muslim Arab husband's machismo, but, since she lived in another country, we could not help her.

The above situations repeated again and again, since many Cuban young women wanted to get away from the Cuban communist system, and one legal way to achieve it was through marrying a foreigner. Most of them were unaware of Muslim traditons because, when in the West, some Muslim Arab men behave differently. They deceive women who are not told or explained clearly about their strict religious customs. Then, on arriving in the Muslim country, their rigorous traditions are applied and a cultural shock takes place.

There are women who, living in the West, fall in love with a Muslim and convert to Islam and use Islamic clothing. Some say they consider themselves happy and not discriminated or ill treated. It is obvious that it is not the same for a converted woman to live a Muslim euphemism in a Western country away from family and the Muslim's country fanaticism, as being immersed in the Muslim traditional society, where all laws and traditions within the core of all the family and society are harsher and mandatory.

I must recognize Lester was a good leader and treated the staff well; he was available all the time. He also had a special personality and intuition for conspiracies, which was in keeping with the relations with Palestinians and other political organizations.

Shortly afterwards, a message from the Division of Cadres and Personnel arrived, stating I had been promoted to Second Secretary and that I would take the vacant position of First Secretary in the staff. Then what Lester did was accredit me before the Syrian government and the diplomatic corps as First Secretary, which improved the vacuum in the chain of command I referred to above.

With the presence of Ambassador Lester Rodriguez and the new Military, Naval, and Air attaché, Lieutenant Colonel Miguel Barreiro, we started to hold meetings very early in the mornings to read and analyze the daily news.

The meetings were held in my office and on my way to the embassy, I would pick up the Cuban student sent by the Foreign Ministry, Orlando Requeijo, so he could take part in them before going to his Arabic class. In addition to that, I explained to Requeijo some daily procedures and tasks, but in a limited way because I never received either any instructions or specific plan for his training or clearance to have him get access to classified information.

Orlando Requeijo was a young man who had a good cultural background and mastered French. He graduated from the High Institute of International Relations four generations after mine. Once he finished his courses on Arabic in Syria in 1986 and started to work for the Foreign Ministry in Havana, he had a skyrocketing career.

Requeijo started working as a specialist for the Division of North Africa and the Middle East in the Foreign Ministry. He was appointed Ambassador of Cuba in Qatar from 1994 to 1998; Director of Foreign Ministry North Africa and Middle East Division from 1998 to 2001; Ambassador and Permanent Representative of Cuba before the United Nations from 2004 to 2006; Deputy Minister of Foreign Relations for Foreign Investment and Economic Cooperation until 2008; Cuban Ambassador in France in 2009; and Cuban Ambassador in Saudi Arabia in 2017.

Another Cuban student of Arabic in Syria called Armando Vergara Bueno, sent by the Foreign Trade Ministry, held the position of General Secretary of the Communist Youth League in the Cuban Embassy in Damascus. In November 2007, Vergara was accredited as Cuban Ambassador in Qatar. I suppose his appointment must have been influenced by his personal relations with his classmate in the Arabic courses in Syria, Orlando Requeijo, who was already Foreign Affairs Deputy Minister on that time, and had been previously Ambassador to that same country.

CHAPTER VII

Alleged Defection Of a CIA Officer

1982

The Republic of Lebanon is the Arab country, where most of the Palestinian forces settled after being expelled from the Hashemite Kingdom of Jordan during the so-called "Black September" in 1970.

During the Israeli invasion of Lebanon in 1982, a Cuban undercover special agent, who contacted only the Ambassador and me (second in charge of the mission), traveled to Syria. To my surprise, he did not get in touch with the military attaché.

Following orders from Havana, I connected the Cuban secret agent with the Democratic Front for the Liberation of Palestine as a Cuban "journalist". I requested them that he was given access to the Beqaa in Lebanon and were infiltrated within the Palestinian forces to watch the pace of confrontation against Israel, so Cuba could acquire "experiences" on what was going on the field. I also asked them to get me a real sample of an armored vest and a helmet used by the Israeli army, since Cuba wanted to take a close look at them. Such "Journalist" returned to Cuba without neither one of us knowing his real name nor what specific department he worked for.

When I was handed the armored vest used by the Israelis, the Palestinians then told me that the vest was hard to find by their snipers because they were used only by Israeli military officers and not by a private. By the way, I remember back at that time, vests were very heavy because I lifted it and personally took it to the embassy.

The Israeli forces, for the first time, had managed to besiege and occupy all Palestinian refugee camps in central Beirut and the Beqaa. A ceasefire was brought about through an international agreement, and the Palestinian resistance was allowed to be evacuated by sea, with every guerrilla fighter carrying a personal weapon and a rifle. The fighters were dispersed through different countries.

One of the Palestinians who recently arrived in Syria from Beirut, whom I had met during one of my trips to Lebanon, handed me a Persian cat and asked me to please look after it for a week while he was being settled. The poor cat almost died because I had forgotten it was inside the car trunk and when I went looking for it, it was soaking wet in sweat.

Mirita, who loves cats, took the cat to her office, and looked after it. Later on, Maitelis was having fun at home playing with the cat, but Mirita noticed a long scar in the cat's belly which seemed odd to her.

When the Palestinian friend came back to pick his cat up, I asked him about the cause of such a scar, and he told me that most of Palestinian files had fallen into Israeli hands in Beirut, so they had come up with the idea of taking out some important documents in different ways, one of them being by inserting an electronic memory or microfilm in the cat's belly through surgery. He apologized for not having told me before, but he had contacted me due to the confidence he had found in the support the brotherly Cubans were giving to the Palestinian cause.

According to some studies on the Middle East, the only people in that region who can be compared, as far as preparation and intelligence goes, to the Israelis are precisely their biggest enemy: the Palestinian people, who have cared to develop professionals in European universities, as well as those institutions in Arab countries and the then Soviet bloc countries. Most professionals working in Gulf countries, such as Kuwait, Saudi Arabia, the United Arab Emirates, etc., are of Palestinian origin.

I received a message at the embassy from one of the trustworthy Palestinian translators, which read that "Jacinto's Friend" was expecting us at the office of the Democratic Front for the Liberation of Palestine.

I did not know what that was about despite the fact it was an organization we had good relations with. I showed up at the FDLP offices, and after exchanging greetings, I was ushered to a salon where we had the traditional "chai" (tea). These offices were situated in the basement of a place in

Northern Damascus, and the salon where we were sitting was dark but spacious. There were four standing fans, each in every corner facing the ceiling, which made us enjoy a pleasant temperature. We sat in a circle-like pattern because there were six Front members, a stranger, and I. There was a momentary silence during which we all looked at each other.

"I'm a friend of Jacinto's", said the stranger breaking the silence in a perfect English.

I realized he was an American by his accent. I also understood this had to do with something important, which was unknown to me.

"Nice to meet you", I told him and remained silent.

The stranger, a little anxious, insisted:

"I'm coming from Beirut on behalf of Jacinto. I thought you knew about it".

"Very well, don't worry. I'm going to contact my ambassador, and I'll be back later", I said succinctly.

I thanked the Palestinian leaders there and told them I would be back in a short while if they allowed me to.

As soon as I got back to the embassy, I personally spoke with Ambassador Lester, who replied he had just received an encoded cable sent by the Cuban ambassador in Beirut, Jacinto Vazquez, stating the code word identifying a CIA officer from Beirut. Such cable pointed out that the Cuban

172

intelligence had prior knowledge about this officer who had wanted to approach Cuba for some time ago.

I returned to the Front's offices, accompanied now by the ambassador and went again through the process taking place in the same salon.

The American again said:

"I come on behalf of Jacinto. I left Beirut evacuated among the Palestinian forces by ship to Syria as if I were just another Palestinian. You can call me Smith".

At that moment, the member of the Front's Politburo, Saleh, gestured, and a rifle was brought to him. Then he asked Mr. Smith in front of us:

"What are you going to do with the rifle you brought?".

"You may keep it", he replied with no further comment.

The Palestinian leader looked at us, and I nodded. As I mentioned above, the Palestinians evacuated by ship from Beirut had been allowed to bring a personal weapon, including a rifle, as part of the ceasefire international agreement with Israel. As Mr. Smith left with the Palestinians posed as one of them, he also brought a rifle which was given to them from the Beirut arsenal.

"Mr. Smith", the ambassador said, "we'll reach out to you in a couple of days and, in the meantime, please, stay with our Palestinian friends. They will treat you well".

The Palestinian leader assured us they would take care of him all the time needed.

Two days later, I welcomed an official from the Cuban Intelligence General Department (known as DGI or G2 in Cuba until 1989, then DI) at the airport, who called himself "Rafael" and said he was one of the specialists in charge of the "Three Letters" (the CIA). The DGI had one of its headquarters in a building located at Linea and A in Vedado, Havana city. Department M1, in charge of United States affairs, took up floors seven, eight, and nine in the building. The "Three Letters" was an undercover encoded way to refer to the CIA.

That night, I invited Mr. Smith for dinner in a restaurant. I picked him up near an apartment building where the Palestinians were living, and I introduced him to Rafael, the Cuban DGI official.

During dinner, Rafael said:

"I have come over from Havana to specially attend to you, and from now on, I'll be a sort of a "Babysitter" for you".

That was a term taken from the Americans by the Cuban officer: a metaphor which meant that Rafael would be taking care of all the details concerning Mr. Smith's needs.

"I can't enter Syria on an official basis", Smith clarified, "because I have some old stuff pending with Ali Duba. Therefore, I can't leave through this country's airport. Ali Duba was the Syrian counterintelligence service chief.

Then Rafael responded:

"I'll manage everything with the Syrians, Mr. Smith, I guarantee your departure".

During that first dinner, we talked about the region's situation in general, and I could realize Mr. Smith was well aware of the intelligence and security structure in these countries. He even knew some of the high-ranking officials personally.

We dropped Smith off near the apartment building where the Palestinians had provided him with lodging. Before saying goodbyes, we told him we would let him know at what time we would pick him up the next day.

Once alone, Rafael told me:

"Tomorrow we'll take Smith to the airport. We'll take the Russian airline Aeroflot via Moscow to Havana. I have already made the reservations. But what this guy doesn't know is that once he gets off the plane in Moscow, we're going to "rough him up", ha, ha, ha", he said sarcastically.

With that gross phrase, the Cuban official hinted they would possibly use some kind of torture to interrogate Smith, which puzzled me because the logical thing was to treat him well if he was really willing to collaborate. But anything could be expected coming from methods used by a communist, brutal, and bloody dictatorship, so I rather remained silent.

Rafael also mentioned that they knew Smith was already a millionaire and, despite that, while working previously as a

CIA officer in several African countries, he had sent signals indicating he wanted to have contacts with Cuba.

"Hector, I need you to find a Cuban diplomatic passport from a member of the Cuban mission with a height similar to Smith's and change the photo with his", Rafael asked me to do. As a norm, I did not ask where he had taken it from.

Smith was about 6'2 feet high, white, with green eyes and black hair.

"There is one detail", I pointed out to Rafael, "the only member with a height similar to Smith's is the radio operator, Echevarria, and his passport shows he has black eyes. This is a small mission with a short staff.

Cuban diplomatic passports state eye color and Echevarria's showed the word "negros" in Spanish.

"It doesn't matter. We must use that one", Rafaele decided, "the photo change and the height info in the passport are more important than what the eye color might tell. Experience has taught me that sometimes you can't try to do things perfectly", Rafael concluded.

The next day I asked captain Echevarria for his passport; he was a communication officer of the Interior Ministry's Counterintelligence in charge of the embassy radio plant. He was in charge of radio contact with Havana through Moscow.

I changed Echevarria's photo with that of Smith in the former's passport and I stamped part of the mission official dry seal on the corner of the new photo resembling the ones In Cuban passports. Echevarria had the rank of diplomatic attaché.

(See below far back in the photo Cuban Diplomatic Attache Ramon Echevaria)

1981, Damascus. Syria. Diplomatic Reception.

Left to right: Mr. Abou Leyla, Member of the Political Bureau of the DFLP; far back Mr. Ramon Echevarria, Cuban Diplomatic Attaché (radio communications operator from the

177

Cuban Intelligence Division); the Author, Mr. Hector G. Aguililla, Cuban Charge D'Affairs a.i.; and Mayor Jose Soto, Cuban Military Attaché.

I drove Cuban agent Rafael and Smith to the airport, but we split up when entering the waiting room. They boarded the same flight to Moscow but separately, as if they did not know each other in order to avoid drawing attention and just in case Smith was recognized.

However, on my way back from the airport to the embassy, I noticed I was being followed by a black car. I slowed down, changed lanes, and then stepped on the gas. I remember I had my pistol in the glove department, took it and put it on the seat. That highway from and to the airport had nothing built around yet; there were neither crossroads nor exits. Thus, it was not advisable to stop in a desolate area. I wondered who they were and what they wanted.

The car was a black Range Rover with two people in it. It dangerously got close side by side with my car and I could see they were pointing a gun at me. My reaction was to get close to them and hit them on the side by turning fast and abruptly toward them. I got the better part at that moment because they could not shoot me, and the Range Rover passenger's gun fell out of his hand when their car was suddenly forced out of the highway. Once I managed to take control of the wheel, I seized the opportunity to put the pedal to the metal and disappear into the city.

I never knew who attacked me, why they did it; I mistrusted even my own people, since I knew about Castro's dictatorship methods. When someone becomes a hindrance for any reason or because he or she knows too much, they are disposed of or have "their health modified". Afterwards, I discarded that idea and thought I was overreacting because that was not my case. Then I supposed they were either Smith's partners or enemies, or a confusion of emotional reaction by someone who had nothing to do with Smith's case. I did not really think it was the CIA because it could no longer act with impunity as it did before, and since they had to abide by the U.S. Congress laws banning operations deemed state terrorism. Anyway, they could have stopped Smith's departure to Moscow. The CIA had already moved to a higher act stage: nothing but intelligence with little violence.

Thus, I thought it probably was an attack attempt or confusion by a terrorist organization that saw me with CIA officer Smith, and maybe they wanted to gun him down thinking he was in my car. Overall, I could never reach a definite conclusion, neither did I give it much thought and it remained an unsolved mystery.

CHAPTER VIII

MISSION IN IRAN

1984

Mirita, for her part, continued to support me on my work and felt very happy over the family we had brought into existence. The only worry she had was our children's future in the totalitarian system implanted in Cuba.

After having been seven years and three months in Damascus, I successfully concluded my mission (December, 1976-March, 1984. I was transferred to the Foreign Ministry in Havana. I had overstayed the average five years the Cuban government sets for a diplomat official overseas. During that time, I could save some hard currency that I then used to buy a car in a government-owned dealer in Cuba.

When I returned to work for the Foreign Ministry I was assigned as a specialist on Iraqi and Egyptian affairs. Mirita continued working for the Foreign Ministry in the Foreign Policy Planning Division.

Soon, we longed for going overseas again to try to get away from the communist system and give our children a better future, freedom, and democracy, but we talked the least needed and with caution for fear of being heard by a hidden mic or someone who could betray us.

One of those days when I felt upset, we were walking outdoors after lunch, and told her:

"Mirita, I can't put up with this farce anymore. Life for me is becoming more unbearable every day in this failed communist system. As a young man, I had the naïve illusion that things would change for the better, that we had to give the system more time, but, on the contrary, everything has gone south. I'm not just referring to the horrible economic disaster, but also to the injustice to the people who are asked to make a greater effort in return for more hunger and lack of freedom. The ones in power have more privilege every day and satisfy their excessive ambitions. Besides, each time, they violate human rights more and more by increasing repression. I definitely believe", I kept telling Mirita, "that for the future of our kids and our own freedom, the best we can do is to go to the United States the first chance we have. I had not talked to you so openly before, although I had wanted to, but I'm at a turning point to start conspiring against the regime".

"I'm very glad you trust me more and more and that you finally decided to talk to me frankly", Mirita said. "I didn't want to put pressure on you and, at the same time, I had my fears, but you know, I got wrapped up with the government because I loved you and wanted to support you in your career. I don't think we should do any crazy stuff against the government, because it would affect your children and me due to the existing surveillance and repression. What I think

181

we should do is wait for the first chance we have when they assign you to a new mission overseas to escape".

"Agreed", I replied, "it seems reasonable. It's a pity we couldn't do it before", I concluded.

Despite our desire to go abroad together again, the next time they sent me away was alone to a temporary mission in Kuwait to replace the second in charge in the Cuban embassy, Roberto Rodriguez, Second Secretary at the time (later to become ambassador in Nigeria, 2010), who went on vacation. In Kuwait, I spent about three months assisting the then ambassador, Jorge Morente, former deputy minister of the Fishing Industry, and former vice director of the Foreign Ministry's North Africa and the Middle East Division.

The water supplied in Kuwait comes from one of the desalination plants in the Persian-Arabian Gulf. Seventy-five percent of the drinking water has to be imported or filtered very well.

Most of the labor was Palestinian, Egyptian, Philippine, Pakistani, Hindu, and other nearby countries. Later on, due to Yasser Arafat's support for Iraq, which invaded Kuwait in 1990-1991, the Palestinians were ejected from Kuwait.

Kwaiti citizens are assigned a generous pension from birth in Kwaiti dinars to live. The government budget has a provision allotted for future generations.

The Kuwaiti capital is very prosperous and has a free market policy where merchandise must have competitive prices.

After I returned to Cuba from Kuwait, I was offered a new temporary mission to another Middle East country, but this time, it was not an Arab country, but a Persian one with Muslim extremist views: the Islamic Republic of Iran, which was at war with Iraq.

The temporary mission was allegedly going to last some three months for me, to substitute then the Cuban Ambassador in Iran, Luis Marisy Figueredo (subsequenty Ambassador in Syria in 2010), but when he returned to Tehran, Marisy arrived with the news that he would be replaced by a new ambassador and my stay had to be extended for two years to cover for the ambassador changes and have someone appointed as second in charge.

When I was initially talked to about the mission in Iran, out of experience, I knew the complications it would bring, since Ambassador Marisy was alone with his wife there. The other Cuban official was a First Secretary who had definitively returned to Cuba a few months back and had still to be replaced.

I requested to have Mirita allowed to go with me to help me as a secretary, because I knew I would need her. But we could not bring the children due to the dangerous situation (Iraq-Iran war), plus the country's conditions, which had recently gone through an Islamic extremist revolution. It was not advisable for obvious reasons, and that is why our children, much to our regret, had to stay in Cuba with one of their aunts and the grandmother looking after them.

When Mirita and I flew in transit through Madrid, we wanted to confirm the Madrid-Frankfurt-Tehran ticket, but the connection flight did not exist because the Federal Republic of Germany had canceled, as a penalty against Iran, flights to that country. So we had to make a new reservation, this time Madrid-Frankfurt-Abu Dhabi-Tehran. It was an exhausting trip, but we had not choice.

Knowing the situation in Iran, where pork and alcoholic beverages are prohibited, we bought a cured pork ham leg in Madrid, six bottles of booze, sausages, and cigarettes. We had no assurance that, despite our diplomatic immunity, we would not be searched and have the goods confiscated on our transit through Abu Dhabi (United Arab Emirates) or on our arrival in Tehran, but we decided to take chances.

In the United Arab Emirates, before going through customs and boarding the plane to Iran, Mirita already had to wear a chador and a veil to be allowed in the Iranian airline despite her diplomatic passport.

A Muslim woman, who was wearing the Iranian attire, searched our carry-ons. I diverted her attention by telling her some words in Arabic that I knew, such as "Helue" (pretty) and "Habibi" (dear), because I was carrying the forbidden goods there. It seems the woman understood and liked what I said, because she smiled at me and blushed while her hands were inside the carry-ons without taking anything out and no objection at all.

In Iran, I had the goods gone through without any setbacks because they incredulously respected my diplomatic passport that time, and our bags were not searched. Maybe they were confident we had already been "Checked" in Abu Dhabi before boarding the Iranian airline plane.

At the airport, no one was there to welcome us due to the unforeseen itinerary change we made in Madrid. I had the embassy's phone number that I had found in the Cuban Foreign Ministry's Iran's files, but we did not have Iranian currency to make a call. I approached someone in military uniform and told him in English we had to make a phone call but I did not have any change. The officer understood and kindly gave me a coin. When I called, someone answered in Farsi (Persian language), and when I asked for the Cuban Ambassador, the one on the other end answered in perfect Spanish that the Cuban embassy had moved. He gladly gave me the new phone number.

I had to ask for another coin and could finally speak with Ambassador Luis Marisy Figueredo, who told me to wait for him, that he would personally go and pick us up immediately.

Twenty-four hours later, I became the mission head as Charge D'Affairs, a.i. In a record time, Marisy handed over the embassy, the residence, my apartment, finances, and management to us. We went over the inventory, including cars. Besides, we drafted and signed all records and documents related to the transfer of duties. Likewise, Ambassador Marisy introduced us to the native staff and put us up to speed concerning the work plan. That night, we did not sleep at all.

The ambassador's haste was due to the fact that he wanted to be in time for his daughter's wedding in Cuba. Due to the delay caused by the issues with our travel itinerary, we had arrived in Tehran three days after schedule.

The Russian Ambassador in Tehran had given Ambassador Marisy the first dog puppy born from a couple selected among the best and biggest Siberian dogs mixed with German Shepherds which had been watching over the Russian embassy. That puppy, named Tribilin, grew way over the average size, and was fed beef, white rice, pasta, raw eggs, and bones. The store for diplomats sold pet food for Tribilin, such as big frozen chunks of beef steaks and large bones.

When Marisy showed us Tribilin for the first time, we were standing on the second floor of the residence next to a stair railing. The dog jumped on Mirita and then on me to greet us, and we almost fell down the stairs due to its weight and strength.

The ambassador's residence occupied the building's second and third floors, while the embassy offices were located on the first one. When Tribilin got loose, it put up a show, since all native employees working in the residence and the native embassy staff started shouting and running or climbing on their desks because they got panicked.

It was interesting to see how Tribilin identified Cubans. When someone arrived, if he or she was Cuban, the dog got cheerful and playfull. However, if the person was from somewhere else, it became aggressive. We could confirm this behavior many times.

The Iranian Ambassador in Cuba, while on vacation in Tehran, and before returning to Havana, visited us at the embassy to make his farewell. When I introduced him to Mirita, she reached out to shake hands, but he stepped back. Mirita insisted again but the Iranian official stepped back again, this time placing his hands in his back. Then I explained to Mirita that the Muslim religion extremists did not allow men to shake hands with women because for them, it is "Haram" (forbiden). This was an example of the Chiite fanaticism in Iran and other Muslim countries, but in Syria, where we stayed for seven years, we never saw such an extremist practice.

According to fundamentalists, women can shake hands with a man only if he is "Mahram" (a man whose relationship with a woman does not allow him to marry her, because it would be incest if he did). They must also travel always accompanied by a "Mahram". Even a "mahram" is sorted by categories depending on the familial relationship: by blood (father, brother, son, or grandfather)' by law (father-in-law, son-in-law, stepfather); or by breastfeeding.

When he returned from vacationing in Cuba, Ambassador Luis Marisy came with instructions to notify the Iranian government of his permanent departure, because he would be replaced by a new ambassador and also bid farewell to the diplomatic corps accredited in Tehran.

The new Cuban ambassador assigned to Iran was Isidro Contreras, who had been dismissed from his Domestic Trade Deputy Minister's position in the Cuban government. Contreras was a Navy captain in the prior regime of Fulgencio Batista, but together with the July 26 Movement forces, he took part in an uprising on September 5th 1957, in the Navy's district in Cayo Loco, Cienfuegos. The Cuban government coined that date to commemorate all the anniversaries of the Revolutionary Navy's creation and turned Cayo Loco into a museum.

(See below left the new Cuban Ambassador, Isidro Conreras, appinted to Iran)

1987, Typical Iranian food, sitting shoeless on a rug at an Iranian family home in Tehran, Iran. On the left, the Cuban Ambassador in Iran, Mr. Isidro Contreras; and on the right, the Author, Mr. Hector G. Aguililla.

I had to remain in Tehran throughout the whole transition of ambassador exchanges. First, the farewell process of Luis Marisy, who made it simple for me because he was an experienced professional career diplomat and then the reception and introduction of the new Ambassador Isidro Contreras, who was a political designation and had no diplomatic experience.

That year, I had to arrange and hold a reception on the new anniversary of the Moncada Garrison attack on July 26. A week before the event, the new ambassador, Contreras, arrived. Since he had not presented his credentials yet, according to protocol norms, he had to remain in his room without showing up until an Iranian authority would allowed him to appear in the event.

When the Iranian foreign minister, Rafsanjani, arrived at the reception, I invited him to sit in a separate small room, and asked him if he would permit the new ambassador, Contreras, to be present despite, he had not presented his credentials yet. He said yes; he had nothing against it. I now told Contreras to join us. He was impatient and had already had a couple of vodka shots.

The new ambassador sat near Minister Rafsanjani, who after welcoming and greeting the former, told the ambassador he had plans to travel to Moscow soon to hold meetings with Russian authorities.

Contreras, who besides having had too much alcohol, stuttered a bit, but his worst trait was his vulgar manners. He asked Foreign Minister Rafsanjani directly:

"So you're gonna go to Moscow for "Biznes"? (biznes is a vulgar Americanism in Cuba, meaning dirty business).

I was shocked by what I had heard. I don't know what the Iranian Foreign Minister was translated to in Farsi.

Later on, during Ambassador Contreras' introduction to Tehran's authorities and the diplomatic corps accredited there, as well as the presentation of his credentials, I had to accompany him. He would stand militarily at attention, clicking his heels and posing with a military salute, which looked ridiculous. I had a hard time training and advising this new "ambassador made on the run", not only on the protocol basis, but also on the mission inner work, since everything was new to him.

While visiting the Nicaraguan Ambassador Murillo and his wife, Maria Elena, at their home, the former asked Contreras if he could get him Cuban country music. And Contreras, who had already had a couple of drinks, answered:

"No problem, buddy, that you can find in Cuba by the ton and no one cares about it".

Contreras' wife, Mirtha, who had a higher cultural and educational level than him, spent all the time staring at him and opening her eyes big time to call his attention.

My wife Mirita, jokingly told Mirtha every once in a while:

"You're gonna get a facial paralysis over beckoning Contreras so much".

Iranian TV was not giving us much choices. At the time we had just two video movies called "The Queen of Chantecler" (1962) featuring Sara Montiel, and the other one "Three Days of the Condor" (1975), by Robert Redford. We saw those movies at least five times each during our stay.

Due to alcoholism or lack of awareness, Contreras got constantly sidetracked. Once he sent a letter to the Domestic Trade Ministry, where he had been a deputy minister, asking for computers, a satellite antenna, rice, beans, and a long list of items, and food to be sent to Iran. Besides, he requested to have a satellite, which according to him, was over Africa, oriented toward Iran to get Cuban TV channels. Mirita and I spent a whole week laughing when we learned about it, and even his wife Mirtha, too.

It happened that he received some of the things he had requested from his former ministry, but, of course, neither computers nor satellite antenna, which were in their initial stages in Cuba, were sent.

When the Domestic Trade Ministry billed the Foreign Ministry for those expenses, the Economic Division reprimanded Contreras, and during his vacation in Cuba, he was summoned by a deputy minister to explain the reasons for the expenses incurred by him without a prior authorization by the Foreign Ministry.

In Iran, despite diplomatic immunity and international law, women from the diplomatic corps were forced to observe the Muslim extremist rules concerning their looks when going out. They had to wear the chador on top of their clothes, a head-scarf covering their hair and forehead (the latter was considered a woman's very sexy look); they could not wear cosmetics on the face or fingernails; they had to wear solid color stockings and close-toed shoes, etc. If they did not respect those regulations, they ran the risk of having acid thrown on their faces or being taken away for whipping.

Loud music is forbidden; only religious or instrumental music is allowed. Alcoholic drinks are also prohibited, although they are made and sold in the black market.

Religion allows for temporary marriages and men always have the primary right for the child custody or parental rights.

I visited the Russian embassy in Tehran several times. It was huge and was surrounded by a double fence where packs of German Shepherds mixed with Siberian huskies walked to watch over it. It had a historic hall that I had the pleasure to visit, where Stalin, Roosevelt, and Churchill met to agree on "D-Day" or the allied troops landing in Normandy on June 6th, 1944, when the total defeat of Germany in World War II began.

The Venezuelan Ambassador, Rafael Zanoni, and his Counselor, Raidi, had good relations with Marisy, and after he left to Cuba for good, they strenghtened their relations with his successor, Contreras, and me, even more. An example of this was the fact that they provided us with the press summaries they made in their embassy.

One of the Venezuelan secretaries, married to an Iranian, who had studied together with her in the United States, provided us with the contact to illegaly exchange hard currency in the black market for Iranian currency. The money value amazingly multiplied by ten as compared to the official Iranian rial exchange. I did this on a monthly basis and not only changed the amount tallyng our salaries, but also part of the mission's budget corresponding to diplomatic events or protocol expenses.

I eventually used other contacts in a jewelry store in Tehran downtown, which the wife of a Bulgarian trade attaché told me about. I always carried a handgun with me when exchanging money. We had received unwritten authorization by the Cuban Foreign Ministry through the ambassador specifying how "not to get our top authorities, in particular Fidel Castro, involved".

Socialist bloc diplomats, as tradition was, gave me a lot of important and confidential information. After one of the monthly meetings, where vodka was aplenty, I was driving back home when something foolish happened. I sped uphill and after reaching the top, I went downhill fast and, unexpectedly, faced a curve with a red light junction. I tried to step hard on the brakes, but the car spinned around 360 degrees in the middle of traffic while another car was turning left. I could finally stop the car right in the junction without colliding with anyone. But where this happened, there were several police officers and patrol cars. A police officer approached me, and I quickly thought: no accident; the alcohol influence; the worries about Mirita being alone at the house waiting for me; the fear of the repressive forces of a fundamentalist government; and the protection my diplomatic immunity I enjoyed; so my immediate reaction was to unjustifiably flee. I was chased by two Iranian Mercedes-Benz police cars. I had a good lead because of my unexpected runaway; then I thought about making a U-turn to return on the opposite lane to outwit them after a curve where I could not be seen, but the road was narrow, and I could not do it at that speed, since the room to turn in the median strip to the opposite lanes was short and narrow. I reached another stop light, in red also, with a line of cars waiting for the light to change. I then turned on a mandatory left after a forced halt, and, at that moment, the patrol cars caught up with me.

About four police officers got out and pointed their guns at me. The sergeant walked in front of my car to check the plates, and after rolling the window down, I slowly and carefully took out my Iranian diplomatic ID from my suit pocket, looking at all times at the officer next to my window, pointing his gun straight to my head. I told them I was a diplomat and they must have mistaken my car for another one. The sergeant looking at my plates approached me very upset and told me something in Farsi signaling me to move on and to the officer to back down. It had been an unnecessary and irresponsible jeopardy that could have cost my life because Iran was at war with Iraq, and they could have thought I was an Iraqi agent running away or any other assumption.

In Tehran, one of my best sources of information came from the Romanian Minister-Counselor, who had been in the city for a long time and had good relations with capitalist diplomats. His ambassador was the dean (ambassador with the longest tenure) of the diplomatic corps and both had arrived at the same time.

In the years 1986-1987, a French delegation visited Iran to negotiate the secret sale of weapons to the highest Iranian levels in government. The Romanian Minister-Counselor obtained all the confidential information on those talks through the French Charge D'Affairs. To my surprise, he gave me all the information on the talks in detail, from A to Z. I sent a special report to Havana, and afterwards, I received, for the first time, a congratulatory letter from the Party's Central Committee.

Likewise, my Romanian "friend" put me up to speed on a secret visit by an American delegation comprised of the National Security Council advisor, Robert McFarlane, and another member of the Council, Lieutenant Colonel, Oliver North, to secretly sell weapons to Iran, finance the Nicaraguan "Contras", and get the release of the American hostages in Lebanon held by pro-Iranian forces.

All that took place during the Iraq-Iran war. Because the sale of weapons to Iran and financing the so-called Nicaraguan "Contras" (opposed to the Sandinista regime) was banned by the U.S. Senate, an investigative committee and a political process called Irangate during Ronald Reagan's presidency were set up. Security adviser Robert McFarlane committed suicide. Oliver North's charges against him were dropped thanks to an immunity agreement warranted over his public testimony in Congress.

In Iran, there was a state of barbarity. The mission's Iranian driver, Samir, had improperly parked several times in front of a post office and one day called me to the embassy saying he had been arrested. His car with diplomatic plates had been towed, and he would neither be released nor the embassy car returned until I showed up at the "Pasdaranes" (security forces) headquarters. I called Iran's Foreign Ministry's Protocol Division, and I was told they could do nothing to intercede before such security forces, that I had better go there if they were requesting my presence. I showed up at the Pasdaranes headquarters, where they asked me for my ID and then told me to sit down and wait. After a long while, an officer appeared and motioned me to go and sit facing a desk. I explained to him in English that I had come for my driver and the car and I wanted to know what exactly had happened. The officer hardly knew English, and we could not understood each other. Finally, another tall and stout Iranian officer popped up, accompanied by two other guards. The one behind the desk gestured to follow him. He took me to a dark room without furniture, and the strong officer stood in front of me in a combat posture without saying a word, surrounded by the rest, I took an on-guard pose, tense, alert to any movement by the alleged opponent, without making either any abrupt, significant, or provocative moves or showing fear waiting to see what would happen. Then, after a brief silence and strain, the guard moved away silently and I was ordered to sit back again fronting the desk.

Since I was not attacked, I realized that what they wanted was to frighten me, but since they could not bring it to fruition, I plucked up courage, and speaking with a strong voice and banging on the desk, I reversed course by telling them they also had an ambassador in Cuba and that what happened to me would happen to him in Havana, too, out of reciprocity. That I could not explain what was going on because Fidel Castro was President Khamenei's and Ayatollah Khomeini's friend, the latter being Iran's supreme leader at the time. But I was never either given answers or a clear conclusion on the situation.

I eventually managed to get my diplomatic ID back, the driver released, and the car returned, Then they let me go. I had to walk several blocks because all the area was blocked to traffic and heavily guarded.

The only logical explanation I found on this incident was that they wanted to scare me, maybe to ask for my collaboration or to reciprocate any hostile action the Cuban intelligence could have taken against the Iranian representative in Havana but, when they saw my tough and resolved stance, they quit trying.

Another incident we went through was when we went out one night to a diplomatic reception in Tehran and were on our way back home. A jeep with two passengers got close to our vehicle on the co-pilot side and pointed their guns at us and gesturing at Mirita's head. Then I realized Mirita's coat hood to cover her hair had slipped back, I immediately told her about it and when she fixed her hair under the hood, they moved on.

It was incredible to know that part of these repressive patrol cars was devoted to demand the strict use of women's Islamic clothing rurles, even to foreigners and even to diplomatic women.

In Iran, what helped us to endure the tense situation was the friendly relations we had with Venezuelans and their families, with which we constantly shared lunch, dinner, and off-the-record meetings. Also, Nicaraguan Ambassador, Mr. Murillo and his wife, visited us and vice versa, although not so often. The Nicaraguan ambassador, whose first name I cannot remember, is the brother of Rosa Murillo, President Daniel Ortega's wife. Nepotism in Nicaragua repeats itself in government positions like in Cuba.

We also made friends with a very pleasant married couple from Armenia, who lived in Tehran, spoke Spanish, and had U.S. residence, a country they traveled to every year in order not to lose their permanent residence status. They ran an oil machinery spare part sales business. They also gave us vodka bottles they got in the black market every once in a while, and they were always very respectful to us and never showed any particular interest except for getting a tourist visa to visit Cuba, which was something we could easily issue with little requirements. Maybe they worked for the Iranian intelligence or, who knows, even for the CIA, but that was just speculation. Once, when Mirita stayed in Cuba for some months, I was alone in Tehran and went out with the Armenian couple in their car. The three of us were sitting in the front seats, with her in the middle and I had my arm stretched over the seat due to the small room in the car. It was not long when a police officer on a motorcycle made us stop. I got out of the car and showed him my diplomatic ID, but the officer insisted on speaking with the Armenian, since it was an infraction to have two men sitting with a woman in the middle.

The Armenian asked me to let him be alone with the officer and moved away a little to speak with him. I have no idea what he told the officer or whether he bribed him, but everything was settled and we continued along the road.

In Tehran, there was a system of ancient aqueducts that still worked. On both sides of the road, there were open canals where wastewater flowed. There was always the danger of falling into the ditches when parking, although

Iranians were used to it. Once, when parking my car, an accident happened: a wheel got into the canal. After we got out of the car, some people volunteered to help, and without asking, they sat on the car fenders, which were on the side of the wheels on the pavement, and in up and down motions, they managed to lift the stuck wheel to the pavement. It looked like routine for them, whom I thanked and moved on.

Since Iran was at war with Iraq, we occasionally had to look for shelter in the embassy basement when the siren went off to warn about a bombing. But due to Tehran being so far from the border, the Iraqi Russian-made jets did not have enough fuel before reaching the city and returning, thus, bombings took place in the outskirts of the city.

Iranian Shiites, even during war, celebrated Ashura festivities in January every year, on the tenth day of the first month, a month called Muharram (holy month) in the Shiite calendar. During those processions, they would hit their heads or whipped their backs and the whole body with chains until they bled. These demonstrations are held to commemorate the martyrdom of the third Shiite Imam, Hussein, grandson of prophet Muhammad.

On the tenth day of Muharram of year 61 of Hijra (pilgrimage to Mecca), October 10th, 680 in the Christian calendar, there was a battle in the city of Kerbala (at present in Iraq), where Shiites and Sunnites split. It is called Ashura because it came from the Arabic word "Ashara", which means number ten.

When we received news of our return to Havana for good, we packed and had to send the bags to the Iranian Foreign Ministry Protocol Division first with a list of contents to be checked, sealed, and sent to the airport. According to their explanation, that was done to avoid smuggling valuable Persian rugs by diplomats, since they only allowed one per diplomat.

During checking one of our bags, a white powder came out, which put the Iranians authorities on the alert, thinking it was a drug or an explosive, but they could verify it was laundry washing powder Mirita had included due to its shortage in Cuba.

After being almost three years in Tehran, we returned to Cuba this time very happy to be able to leave that unsafe and troubled place. On boarding the plane, we had the impression we were waking up from a nightmare. Above all, we were lucky and happy to be reunited with our two children, Maitelis and Eddy. The separation might have caused traumas or emotional burdens to our kids or even to ourselves.

Maitelis was already studying in Havana, in Santa Fe middle school to where she had to take the bus to come and go because, in the town of Jaimanitas, where the kids were being looked after by their grandmothers, there was no middle school. She had excelled in class and social activities there.

Eddy was still in Havana, in Jaimanitas elementary school and had also shined in class and sports. He liked track sprints, swimming, and karate. Teachers and principals of both kids had a very good opinion about them.

Maitelis had a bicycle accident when one foot tangled up in a wheel, but there were no further aftereffects. Eddy also hit his head, but it turned out to be a minor injury; he was assisted by a doctor friend of mine living in the neighborhood.

One day, Mirita and I were walking by the only movie theater in the neighborhood and saw our son Eddy, 9 at the time, with one arm over a girl's shoulder. We did not say anything to him, and kept walking laughing. Later on, we asked him whether that girl was his girlfriend, and he told us she lived across the street from the movie theater. We warned him there could be trouble for him if her parents saw them together just like we did, but he retorted that they knew where the girl's parents were and the time they returned home.

Mirita and I were astonished over the kids' slyness at such young age, but since it had to do with the boy, I was proud of it and did not reprimand him. However, I suppose I would have a different stance if it had had to do with my daughter due to our cultural habits.

CHAPTER IX

PLANS TO FLEE CUBA

1985

Our family's happiness, just like most in the Cuban population, felt overshadowed by the lack of freedom and opportunities for a better future. We had to live under the same roof packed together with our relatives due to the house shortage, facing major problems with public transportation, staples, and other basic needs.

Just like many Cuban institutions, the Foreign Ministry, utilizing its own labor, shaped a "Microbrigade" for the construction of buildings aimed at easing the housing needs.

International Relations' Higher Institute students worked forty-five days a year constructing a building ever since its foundations were laid. Prior to that, we spent forty-five days a year in the sugar cane fields.

After graduation, we went once a week to continue the building construction with the microbrigade just like all Foreign Minister officials and another fifteen days annually. We worked with the micro brigade ever since construction started for three straight years, until I was assigned to a mission overseas, and despite that, I did not have an apartment from the building allotted for me. Priority was given to seniors with a long revolutionary history, to others over cronyism, and to a group of Latin American guerrilla fighters living in Cuba as refugees.

During assembly meetings to pick the candidates to get such apartments, the participants criticized each other unscrupulously. They took out the dirty landry to spoil each other's images. It was a fight with abjections among themselves with the intention to have an apartment assigned to them.

I feared that my position in the Ministry could eventually end up in crisis and that I would face serious difficulties due to my opinions and arguments in the political ideology field. I had already been heavily criticized over having "Ideological Biases".

When working abroad, I met several high-ranking officials like Rene Rodriguez Cruz, at the time member of the Party's Central Committee and President of the Cuban Institute of Friendship with the Peoples, considered one of the ideologues within the party.

Rene had an arrest warrant since 1982 in the United States for drug trafficking. He asked me to exchange currency in the black market and serve him as a tourist guide for several days without taking into account, how much work I had and how busy I was. I was lucky to see that he got dizzy several times in my car, and he did not like the way I drove in the old and new Damascus.

Also, Commander Guillermo Garcia Frias, a Politburo member, exchanged money illegally and bought one of the most expensive white suits he later used to wear.

Likewise, Mrs.Vilma Espin, Raul Castro's wife and Chairwoman of the Cuban Women's Federation, bought a pair of the finest high-top boots and another pair for her daughter Deborah, who was accompanying her, plus genuine leather coats for both, curtains for her house in Cuba, and five olive oil cans of five gallons each. She used the money the embassy female staff had collected out of their pockets monthly to donate to the Cuban Women's Federation organization for her to make those purchases.

Lastly, I learned that the Cuban military attaché accredited in Syria at the time, Lieutenant Colonel Miguel Barreiro, also took to Cuba during his vacation two cans of high-quality Syrian olive oil of five gallons each earmarked for the Commander-in-Chief, Fidel Castro himself. According to comments Lieutenant Colonel Barreiro made to me, after struggling with and looking after the two big cans of oil during his vacation trip with his family from Damascus, with flight connections in Rome and Madrid until he landed in Havana airport, an officer of Fidel's bodyguard squad picked the cans up without even thanking him.

We were already resolved to abandon the abominable and failed socialist system in Cuba, so for several months, we made plans to escape, but always thinking of fleeing together: Mirita, my two kids, and me.

While walking at night in the Jaimanistas neighborhood where we lived, we took the time to talk about the desire we had to leave the island. When we walked down the shoreline, and looked at the sea, we thought of the possibility of buying or hijacking a boat to vanish.

My brother-in-law, Francisco Chaviano, who was always openly opposed to the Cuban regime, would join us in our desire to leave Cuba then.

In the Jaimanitas River mouth, there was a so-called fishing cooperative and a coast guard unit on one side, and the Marina Hemingway on the other side. There were boats on both sides all the time and we knew how to get to them, not only by land but by sea also. Of atmost importance was to get to know the coast guard movements.

Marina Hemingway, adjacent to Jaiimanitas beach in Havana.

There came a time when I told my brother-in-law Frank about the option to create an organization to fight the regime, but he advocated for doing it by joining the human rights activists peacefully. I rather faced them with a more radical organization of my own. I said to Frank that my father used to say that "it is better to be a mouse's head than a lion's tail", and that was why we should found our own organization with an action plan.

Nonetheless, I expressed to him that if the occasion to leave on a new official mission abroad with my family arose, I would take it to run away from the regime- an idea he agreed with.

On a trip to Varadero Beach, we rented a boat for fun. Frank, my sister Anita, her children, Mirita, my children, and I were aboard the boat. We started rowing away from the shore. We felt a kind of euphoria with the desire to continue to point the bow towards Florida, but we knew the boat was not safe enough for the family, with five kids on board.

Soon, a coast guard boat came into sight near us without issuing any warning, but we understood that they were watching us. We rowed back to the shore with frustration, after having lived a couple of volatile emotional moments dreaming of freedom.

Before long, I was offered two choices to go to African countries for a permanent post as First Secretary and Second in Charge of the mission. One was in an English-speaking country, Tanzania, and the other one in a French-speaking country, Madagascar. As my second language was French, I did not hesitate to choose Madagascar.

There was just a big inconvenience: Maitelis had finished elementary school, and there was a regulation stating that "children of officials in secondary school would not go abroad to avoid a possible ideological bias". This implied that Mirita and I had to make make-shift moves because we had made the decision to whether flee Cuba together or not. With that purpose in mind, I invited the Foreign Minister's Cadre and Personnel Department director, Luis Marisy Figueredo, who had been our ambassador in Iran, for dinner. I had substituted Marisy in Tehran when he went on vacation and later substituted him again when he finished his mission and a new ambassador was appointed.

Marisy's wife, Carmen, and Mirita joined us at the restaurant "The Arab" in Havana. There we took the opportunity to ask Marisy for his support for us to be able to take Maitelis to study at the French Lyceum in Madagascar. Marisy suggested that I wrote a letter to Minister Isidoro Malmierca so my daughter's case could be discussed for approval by the Council of Ministers as an exception in a meeting where he would support the request endorsement. In those Council meetings, directors, deputy ministers, and general secretaries of the Party, the Youth Communist League, and the Unions, took part.

Mirita also asked Deputy minister, Pedro Diaz, who was very close to the minister, for his support. She had already worked for him some time ago. We gave him good video movies we had brought from abroad that were not available in Cuba in order to gain his support. Likewise, Mirita requested the support of Ignacio de Armas, Foreign Policy Planning Division Director, where she worked before our departure.

Later on, I spoke with my director, the deputy minister of my division, and the general secretaries of the Party, the Youth Communist League, and the Unions, requesting the same support.

We had the endorsement of at least eight votes with great influence on our favor in the Council. I counted on the prestige of my work resume, and I was well-known personally by the Minister himself. Furthermore, his personal secretary, Oscar, had worked with me in Syria, where he was the personal secretary of Ambassador Barber, which somehow helped a little. Besides, I clearly argued in my letter the negative consequences it brought about the separation of children from their parents, something that had taken place before: Maitelis was suffering from alopecia as a consequence and likely psychological traumas, plus the fact that my parents were old and could not look after them like before, etc.

We finally achieved our goal. The Council of Ministers, based on the arguments stated in my letter, and the lobbying by Mirita and I, unanimously passed in their meeting in June 1988, the exception for our daughter Maitelis to be able to travel with us overseas.

Since my son Eddy was a small child, we had no difficulties concerning him, and he was going to be enrolled in the same French school in Madagascar.

After the kids' green light to fly, we obtained their grade transcripts, birth certificates, and international vaccine records. In the case of Mirita and I, we did not request our birth and marriage certificates to avoid drawing any attention. The latter were later sent to us by our relatives in Cuba to the United States.

During all that process prior to our departure, besides the official training I had to fulfill to a T to avoid suspicions, I was going through other parallel arrangements, personal and secret, to escape from the regime.

I did some research on how the relations between Cuba and Spain were during a friendly talk with the then Spain specialist, Carlos Owen, who had been my classmate. He told me, among other things, that an immigration agreement between Cuba and Spain existed or was brewing to deport the Cubans who illegally stayed in that country.

I personally would have rather stayed in Spain because I liked that country in general and there were cultural and blood ties. But, unfortunately, even though I visited it on a legal basis, the existence of left-wing forcers connected with the Cuban nomenklatura was substantial, so I deemed it safer my family and me to apply for asylum in the American embassy. Moreover, we both my wife and I had relatives living in the United States, while we had zero relatives in Spain at that point.

We gathered addresses, names, and phone numbers of our relatives in the United States through our relatives in Cuba. We also collected operational information in Madrid, such as the address and phone number of the U.S. embassy, the Ambassador's name, the hotel location from where we would escape, and a map.

I was once at the Ministry's library (we still had no internet) searching for information on the United States embassy in Madrid when I saw the general secretary (Hidalgo) of the Party's Division I worked for come in. I had with me other books related to Madagascar in case something like that occurred. Hidalgo approached me and asked me:

"Aguillilla, how's that training going?"

I tried to pretend I was very focused on my reading and replied:

"Very well, thank you. Trying to make good use of the little time I have left."

Then he went looking for a book and left. I was logically afraid to be exposed and have all the plans go south.

I had developed many hand blisters due to the stress during that training to travel; study the country I was appointed to go; meetings with other state institutions and leaders of the Foreign Ministry itself; attend conferences;

overview of staff norms and protocol abroad; departure paperwork; and our own secret plans to flee.

I tried to hide the blisters because any keen eye of a knowledgeable person could raise suspicions seeing them, since this was a proven symptom of excess adrenaline in people who want to escape or desert.

We finally departed all together on October 10th 1988, via Madrid, Spain, allegedly headed to Madagascar. No one thought we had plans, kept in absolute secrecy, of deserting from the tyranny searching for freedom, democracy, and a better future for our children. Only two persons knew about our intentions the day before. One was my wife's aunt, Rosa Rodriguez, who was like her mother because she raised Mirita since early childhood, and the other one was my brother-in-law, Francisco Chaviano, who was my accomplice. I told the latter where I had hidden a letter telling my parents the decision I had made. I asked him to hand it over to them with a neighbor doctor friend of mine to be present, just in case my mother was affected by the news.

I had been instructed that during my transit through Madrid, I should accompany an official from my department, Mr. Prieto, and his wife, who would be traveling for a mission abroad for the first time. I had precisely trained Prieto for his mission because he had been assigned to Iran, where I had worked. Prieto was a member of the Communist Party, which neither Mirita nor I were members of. Before reaching the age limit in the Youth Communist League, Mirita resigned from its membership and was never gone through the vetting process to be a Communist Party member. In my case, I did not resign due to my work position, but when I went through the vetting process, I did not meet the necessary requirements to be a member due to ideological bias. That was due to my occasional opinions and display against some of the party lines.

To be assigned as the second in charge of a mission, one of the requirements was to be a party member, but they made an exception in my case based on my experience, and work capacity and prestige.

I suspected that Prieto had instructions from the party to keep an eye on me during our transit in Madrid, since over the last few years, due to the difference of opinions with extremist communists, I had been criticized for having alleged "Ideological Biases", but I had an edge thanks to my experience and knowledge on the field to fool them because I had already been in transit through Madrid about twenty times. And, to top it all, in the Havana-Madrid flight, was my then director, Ulises Estrada (the black panther), who said he was taking part in a joint committee of cooperation between Cuba and Algeria.

A few days before the departure date, I had been summoned by Colonel Labrador to his office for a meeting. He was the head of the Foreign Ministry's Department One.

That department has an office in the Foreign Ministry's building created as a representation of the Armed Forces Intelligence to coordinate their interests with those of the officials of diplomatic agents.

In Cuba, at the beginning of the so-called Special Period, the military presence in most of the state civil institutions increased.

"Comrade Aguililla: the colonel told me, "It's good you came to my meeting. We have pleasant memories of your prior cooperation with our ministry and, on this occasion, we also need it again. We don't have a military attaché nor any other member of our military intelligence apparatus in Madagascar for being such a small embassy. But let me take this moment to clear something out: Why are you flying through Madrid and stay there for three days and not fly through Moscow?"

"Colonel", I jumped in, "I'm flying via Madrid because I have already been assigned a new set of clothes for me and my family to purchase, according to the Foreign Ministry's Norms and Procedures Manual. That's why I have three days in transit; besides, that is the best route for a connection from Havana to an African country. Do you have any questions about it?"

"No, none at all", the colonel said, 'it was just out of curiosity because we have all the confidence in you, and I wanted to confirm those were the reasons".

"I'd never leave without seeing you, colonel", I pointed out. "Tell me what your goals and interests are and I'll take care of them".

"Very well, comrade Aguililla, I invite you to watch a video we are going to show in the theater this afternoon to the heads of missions who are here on vacation", Labrador said, "General Luis Barreiros, head of the Intelligence General Division, will explain to you all about the large amount of officials, who have deserted and the recommendations to avoid that. I'll be waiting for you without delay."

"Yes, of course, I'll be there", I answered. I was brief in order to end the meeting quickly, but the colonel added:

"About Madagascar precisely, the instructions are to gather any information on the Americans, French, and UN navies moving or staying in the Indian Ocean. Also, French or American presence and military advisory in that country, plus the general directions you already know. We have a great battle of influences in that country with the United States, and I think you are the right person for this mission".

"I'll take it into account very well", I told him, "it's understood. We'll see each other in the afternoon if you don't have further questions".

"OK. That's all. See you in the theater at 17:00, don't forget it is very important", he concluded.

217

I left a little tense because Colonel Labrador had been the only person who had directly questioned my days in transit in Madrid, but it seems it was only his old wolf-hunting instincts. They always tried to make the officials had their flight connections in socialist bloc countries, mainly Moscow, Prague, or Berlin.

During the meeting, I was invited to participate together with the heads of missions, General German Barreiros Caramé (Luis), head of the General Intelligence Division, talked about the increasing number of officials that had deserted and the measures to be taken to avoid this from happening, among them, not to strongly criticize or penalize an official while overseas.

He also showed a video on the recent U.S. military air attack against Lybia and President Muammar El Khadafi's home. It was a computerized replica of the whole operation, from where the U.S. warplanes took off, the route they took, the rocket targets, and the planes' return.

Besides, General Barreiros referred to the Special Plan for the Special Period, pointing out measures and directions the heads of missions had to carry out, among them, to draw up a contingency plan in case of an aggression or general blockade to the Cuban island by the United States in order to be able to survive and continue to work, even independently, if communications were cut off.

A year later, in 1989, Brigade General Luis German Barreiros Caramé, was removed as head of the General Intelligence Division by Fidel Castro. He was replaced by Division General Jesus Bermudez Cutiño, who was head of the Armed Forces Military Intelligence for twenty years.

Several high officials of the Interior Ministry were "Involved" in narco-trafficking and were jailed and executed in the so called Causes 1 and 2, when the Armed Forces Division General, Arnaldo Ochoa, was sentenced to death by firing squad.

Everything took place during the period when the Soviet Union, which was one of the main sources of strategic information on the United States, collapsed.

Meanwhile, in May 2001, Fidel Castro made his first official visit to Syria and held meetings with President Bashar El Assad, son of former President, Hafez El Assad, who died a year before.

Fidel was the artifice of connections, support, and training of many terrorists in the Middle East and Latin American by using his relationship with Iraq, Syria, Democratic Yemen, the Palestinians, and lastly, Iran.

Unfortunately, Fidel Castro also relied on the alliance of some Latin American left-wing high-profile figures like Hugo Chavez in Venezuela, Daniel Ortega in Nicaragua, Rafael Correa in Ecuador, Lula da Silva in Brazil, and Tabaré Vazquez in Uruguay.

CHAPTER X

In the United Estate: The CIA and the FBI

1988

After a long flight from Frankfurt and a security run down Maryland highways to avoid being followed, we were accommodated in a beautiful house in a small neighborhood near Andrews Air Base.

The house was well furnished and had two floors plus a basement. The latter had a wide empty space and an a/c, washing machine, dryer, and an iron board.

On the first floor, we found a hall, a dining room, a kitchen, a half bath, and a family room with a chimney facing the backyard and the woods in the back.

On the second floor, you could see three bedrooms and two bathrooms. The master room was wide and had windows with a view to the street and the backyard.

A very nice lady was expecting us at the new home to show Mirita all the house particulars, including the microwave oven usage, which was something new for us at that time (October 28th, 1988).

The woods behind the backyard had fauna, which included deer, squirrels, hares, and a variety of birds, among other animals.

The neighborhood where we were residing was in the suburbs next to where the borders of Maryland, Washington, D.C., and Virginia merged.

Three days after our arrival, on October 31st, Halloween or Witch Night was held in the United States as usual. Someone had already mentioned it, so we bought small candy bags, since that day, neighborhood kids in disguise used to knock on doors saying, "Trick or Treat".

According to a Celtic legend, it was better to treat at whatever cost by giving the kids candies and chocolate; otherwise, the trick would be to curse the house. Actually, today it is held as a tradition for the kids to have fun by wearing costumes and receiving candy without anyone thinking of cursing anybody, let alone for religious reasons. This holiday was our first acclimatization as immigrants to a non-Cuban tradition, to a new culture.

But the funny side was that when the first kids knocked on our door, I feared I would run out of candies, so I put just one candy on each basket until Mirita and the kids saw that and laughed at me, telling me I was making a fool of myself and then we started giving out more. Over the next few years, our children took part in the holiday, and today, even our five grandchildren born in the United States wear costumes saying, "Trick or Treat".

A few weeks after arriving in the United States, we had a new identity with changed names provided by the CIA. We became the "Fernandez" family for several years.

The next new holiday for us was Thanksgiving, held in the United States on the fourth Thursday in November. In general, during this holiday, relatives and friends get together to share an abundant dinner or banquet. The goal is to thank God and your peers while many pray. The main course is roast stuffed turkey. It is served with jelly or redberry sauce. Also served are vegetables, corn, American yellow sweet potato, mashed potatoes with turkey sauce, and the traditional pumpkin pie. The origin of this holiday goes back to the English settlers in the 1620's when about a hundred pilgrims landed in the Massachusetts coast aiming to establish the Plymouth colony, where the harsh winter conditions took them by surprise. Half of them did not survive and the ones who did had to thank the aid and food of native Americans in the area: the Wampanoag. Then the colony governor proclaimed it Thanksgiving Day.

I had my first U.S. driver's license issued a few days before Christmas in Virginia in 1988.

I went to a gun pawn shop and was amazed at how easy it was, at that time, to buy a Westchester Police semiautomatic chromed shotgun with changeable long and short barrel. I also bought a 9 mm Browning handgun, which I knew was very accurate.

When I returned home, I saw a hare in the woods, and I could not resist the temptation to test the shotgun. I half opened the living room glass door, stuck out the barrel and took a shot at about a 100 feet distance and hit the target. I lifted the poor animal which was infested with insects and ticks. I decided to throw it away.

While I went out to work, Mirita stayed home as a housewife teaching the kids English. I often visited Virginia and Washington, D. C. but, above all, the former because it had very pleasant and beautiful places like "Old Town Alexandria". That city was bathed by the Potomac River, with colonial-style buildings and parks, and nice bars and restaurants.

From the Virginia shore you could see take-offs and landings of planes at Ronald Reagan Airport, the Arlington Cemetery, and the Washington Monument. In the fall, the tree leaf colors were beautiful.

During that time, we called some of our relatives using public booth phone coins and visited them in rented cars. They lived in New Jersey, New York State, and Miami, Florida, where we spent our first Christmas with freedom in the United States. All my relatives in Miami gathered in one of my uncle's houses where a pig was roasted for Christmas' Eve in a backyard oven as it was traditional for Cubans.

On our return to Maryland, I was told that the DGSE (French intelligence) had requested an interview with me,

223

which I accepted and held. Amon other things, they were interested in the movements of a couple of their diplomats (French), one in Syria and another in Iran, who had given me information not only to us but also to socialist bloc's countries.

Afterwards, I was offered to have a meeting with the Mossad (Israeli intelligence), but I rejected it despite knowing its efficiency, for considering it, at that time fanatics just like the Palestinians.

Our kids started to attend school and adapt to the new system. They learned English fast and got good grades.

At the end of that period, I had meetings with State Department officials and the national and international press accredited in Washington, D.C. Also, with some Latin American journalists and Cuban exiles, among them Tomas Regalado, who was a Miami commissioner and Mayor, and the famous writer and journalist Carlos Alberto Montaner, who lives in Spain.

I had interview requests by the Florida International University (FIU) and the Cuban American National Foundation, which I declined because I decided to stay away for some time from publicity and to devote myself to rebuild my private family life.

During all that time we lived in Maryland, we were assisted by two CIA agents who we called Bill and James. The former was born in a Caribbean Island, maybe Jamaica, and the latter, James, was an American with British accent because he had lived many years in England. He was always dressed up with a tie and a suit pocket square matching the tie color. Both men were very helpful, polite, and professional.

One night, we invited David, the CIA officer who accompanied us from Germany and had given us a warm and friendly treatment, to dinner. He had kept occasional contact with us.

David was a smart young man, tall, and physically fit because he liked jogging but was insatiable with food, especially sweets. At David's request, Mirita cooked cod with potatoes and crispy shredded beef. He often said, "Cod with Bread" (bacalao con pan, a Cuban saying).

On that occasion, we also invited David's boss, a well-mannered and educated person, who had served in, among other countries, Argentine, so he spoke Spanish, too. During dinner, the situation in Panama was brought up, in particular, the defying attitude of then President Manuel Noriega (December 1988), who had raised a machete during a rally threatening the United States. The CIA high-level official, in a somewhat unpleasant tone, said:

"Hector, you'll see that soon we're going to do something concerning Noriega and Panama, take it for granted."

Exactly a year after that comment, in December 1989, the United States invaded Panama and President Noriega was brought by force to the United States, indicted and jailed.

Shortly before we moved to Florida at the beginning of 1989, thirty-two years ago from today (2021), officer Bill offered me a confidential contract regulating my relationship with the CIA for several years. This contract comprised a set of benefits.

First, Mirita and I thought of moving to West Palm Beach or Fort Lauderdale in South Florida, but we finally made up our minds and moved to Orlando in central Florida. Before leaving Maryland, where we lived for about seven or eight months, CIA agent Bill told me:

"Mr. Hector, you don't owe us anything nor we owe you anything, either. Now you'll move to a new stage, although we'll keep in touch through agent Carlos in Orlando."

I can attest, due to my personal work experience and the treatment to my family and me, the great professionalism of a powerful organization like the CIA, the officers and agents of which were respectful all the time and serious about complying with all their promises and commitments. My family and I are very grateful for their kindness, with which we were treated all the time.

We moved from Maryland to Orlando in Florida. We drove down in my new model car. On our drive through North Carolina, I was given my first ticket for speeding in the United States.

The new car which I chose, a 1989 Mercury Grand Marquis, white with blue interior, was a generous gift from the President of the United States.

In Orlando, Mr. Bill and the new designated contact, Agent Carlos, were waiting for us when we reached the city. We called Bill on the phone, and he gave me directions to the hotel where he was staying. I met him and the new agent at the lobby; the new agent pseudonym was Carlos who, from that moment on, would be our new contact with the CIA and the FBI.

We drove to a tourist community where they had rented a two-story, furnished house for us. The place was a bit expensive so, therefore, we had to try to find where to reside quickly.

After the regular paperwork related to changing my car plates for the new state, we opened bank accounts. We devoted time during the first two weeks to find a place to rent or buy. After visiting more than twenty open houses, we decided to buy under financial conditions, always thinking of being able to sell the day we wanted to go and live somewhere else. Besides, it was convenient due to the tax interest deduction and the value increase with time.

Due to our lack of credit history, we had to give a thirty percent down payment with a rather high interest rate.

At the beginning there were some issues with the bank due to inadequacies when verifying my supposed job, which led me to tell my new contact Carlos the following:

"If the required documentation does not arrive here by 11 a.m. tomorrow, I'll go with my family to Miami. I'm sorry, but this failure creates a great distrust ".

In reality, it had been a minor mistake, but I took advantage of it as a pretext to give him an ultimatum because deep inside, I wished to leave for Miami, which I had not done just to follow their recommendations. But Federal Express delivered the document on time, and I remained in Orlando.

We bought a house in the suburbs by the border between Orlando and Oviedo. Mirita was happy because we had achieved the so-called American dream in record time.

We received the rest of our belongings we had left in Maryland, among them the bicycles we had bought for the kids.

The house had a modern design split into two main wings: on the left, the master room, a bathroom with a double sink, and a large closet with a hallway that led to another room, where we set up an office. The hallway had, in turn, a door through which you could reach the living room, and another door to the terrace. And on the right wing, there were two bedrooms for the kids, a bathroom, and a double roll-up garage door.

In the middle, there was the living room on one side and the family room on the other, split in the middle by a big bar and a half bath with a door to the terrace. The family room had a chimney that was next to the kitchen. The latter had an island with the dining room next to it, where both had a view to the garden. The whole house was surrounded by a vast piece of land.

We bought modern furniture. Mirita decorated the house with wall paintings and curtains while I took care of the swimming pool, mowed the grass, did gardening, and sowed some plants in the backyard.

The kids also enjoyed the new house that included a tennis table in the Florida room, a swimming pool with a springboard, bicycles, and a German Shepherd puppy.

In our new city of residence, Orlando, as part of a logical security process, the FBI counterintelligence spent some time doing some check-ups, including going through a voluntary polygraph test, known also as a "Lying Test", myself twice and Mirita once. It was not a problem for us to accept taking the test because there was no reason to lie or hide anything. In my opinion, these polygraph tests were obsolete. There are many examples of inefficiency like the infiltration of some twenty Cuban double agents in the CIA in the eighties, who passed the test without detecting their lies. It is incredible that the polygraph test is still used in a developed country such as the United States, although its results are gracefully not accepted as evidence in a trial because they could incriminate innocent people.

The police-like process we went through with the FBI was, in general, unpleasant, but not for long. This process did not minimize our gratitude and admiration for this great country, the United States of America, its authorities and institutions.

With great devotion and faith to restart our lives and build a new future in a system new for us, we took the most diverse jobs. Mirita and I started studying accounting.

Among the many jobs and businesses, I had been truck driver, taxi driver, security guard, video sales and rentals, car sales, real estate sales and appraisals, mortgage loan officer, food and drink sales, furniture sales, and stock market investor.

Pursuant to the required paperwork to bring a relative from Cuba to the United States at that time, we sent my parents a letter of invitation on behalf of my now late aunt Lily, RIP, who lived in Miami. We feared the Cuban government would not allow them to travel, but, to our surprise, they did. Then we sent the air tickets, and they arrived in Miami. I asked my now-deceased uncle Meco, RIP, Aunt Lily's husband, to take my parents to a Miami hotel parking lot, where I would be waiting for them. I, of course, asked him not to take them straight to where I was and made sure no one was following them. That he did and then drove them in a rental car to Orlando. On our way from Miami to Orlando down I-95 nearing Cocoa Beach in the Atlantic coast, my father noticed a car was following us.

I exited I-95 on purpose and parked on a mall street right side abruptly. The car following us had to pass by my side and go on. I quickly followed it, took down the car make, model, and plate number. It vanished and never saw it again.

Later on, I reported the car details to my contact Carlos to have them checked by the FBI, and it happened that the car belonged to the FBI itself.

I had already realized once that I had been followed in Orlando. When a car passed me by, I stared at the driver. He signaled me to click my seat belt. I imagined it must have been an undercover police car. Shortly after, I met the driver, who was the head of the FBI office in Orlando, although the headquarters were in Tampa.

We took our parents to visit several Disney World parks and other public parks. We cooked stuff they liked, and we were glad to share several moments together.

Also, while living in Orlando, we filed for the visit of an aunt of my wife's, Rosa Rodriguez, RIP, who raised her since early childhood like a mother. This was done through my wife's relatives in Miami, and we managed to bring her to spend some time with us, too.

A few years later, we moved to Palm Coast near Flagler Beach in Florida, where we rented a house with a canal in the back with access to the ocean, while we had our house in Orlando rented out to a couple.

Palm Coast is a nice place, but most of the inhabitants were retirees and there was no nightlife. The kids got bored and had to travel to a city a bit far away to go to the beach of enjoy social life.

I had already started a video sale and rental business in a town near Palm Coast, called Bunell, where I made a reasonable amount of money because it was the only of its kind there. There was a similar store in Palm Coast and another one in Flagler Beach, which made it the third in the area. But due to demands from my kids, my wife, and my own desire, we decided to sell the business to finally move where we always wanted, Miami, where many of our relatives still live. Like the saying goes in Cuba: "the deer always heads to the woods".

The city of Miami got its name from the Mayaimi native American tribe, and it is located on the Miami river between the Everglades and the Atlantic Ocean.

Miami is now a city with a very mixed population, where there are many Hispanics from several nationalities, but for many years was mostly made up of and developed by Cubans. That is why you can feel a little like in a "democratic Havana".

What is officially called the city of Miami, based on the 2020 census, it had 442,241 inhabitants, but all the metropolitan area had over 2,071,767 in Miami-Dade County.

Cubans in Miami have access to all Cuban typical and traditional consumer products; Spanish is mostly spoken and there is a pluralistic Hispanic cultural environment, including theater, radio, press, and local TV in Spanish. It is said that Miami still is Latin America's capital.

Miami Port is considered the one with the most cruise ship anchored in the world and the headquarters of several cruise companies. Besides, the city has the highest concentration of international banks in the world.

At the beginning, we rented a house in Coral Gables, one of the most distinguished and emblematic places in Miami. Thereafter, we sold the house in Orlando and bought one in the Miami's Southwest.

My parents visited us again from Cuba when we were already living in Miami. Even my two sisters, Isis and Anita, also came to visit us. In 2012, Anita came with her husband, Frank, who left Cuba as a former political prisoner.

My father, who rests in peace, was the first of my parents to pass away in Cuba. My mother, already a widow, came alone to visit Miami, where I managed to have her had heart surgery in one of the best hospitals in the United States. She had a successful surgery, but a few years later passed in Cuba. Of course, I could not attend any of my parents' funeral services for obvious reasons. My departure from

233

Cuba was a trip without return until it becomes a truly free and democratic country.

My children were baptized in Miami because in Cuba, we could not do it as, at that time, we could have lost the possibility to travel overseas.

After I finished my confidential agreement with the CIA, which lasted several years, we voluntarily took our original names back. Later on, we became naturalized American citizens. That was welcomed with great joy and prestige, since we could enjoy all rights an American citizen has, except for being the country's president.

We traveled to places like Bahamas, Grand Cayman, St. Croix, Saint Martin, Jamaica, Honduras, and Mexico on cruise ships because of the benefits my son Eddy had thanks to having worked for some time in the cruise industry. We also visited several U.S. states, including the fantastic city of Las Vegas. We went to several shows, but the one we liked most was that of Siegfried and Roy's white tigers at the Mirage Casino Hotel. They made an elephant disappear just thirty feet in front of us, which was really impressive. Unfortunately, shortly after, a white tiger bit Roy in the neck and dragged him all over the stage in front of the audience. Roy became gravely ill but had a good recovery; today both have passed away for other reasons.

Because my wife likes crab meat so much, on a Mother's Day already in Miami, we had lunch at a seafood restaurant in one of the Florida Keys: Isla Morada. On our way back to Miami in the afternoon, we decided to take a dip at the beach for fun and we ended up in Key Biscayne. In the park, there were three individuals sitting in a car with dark glasses, two whites and a black, who made me feel uneasy, but there was a police officer on horseback near us, and since we only intended to take a quick dip, I made the mistake of leaving our bags with our belongings in the car trunk, including my wife's credit cards, her keys, and one of my guns, which I had in the glove department. When we started to move away from the car, I turned to look at them. I almost turned back, but my wife called me, and I did not go back.

We were in the water for about half an hour and then got back to the car. To our dismay, those guys had stolen the bags in the trunk but not the gun. It seems the individuals I had seen were waiting for a chance and waited for the police officer to go away. They easily broke the trunk lock with a screwdriver. We returned home, filed a police report and called the credit card companies to block the cards. That night my son and I (with guns in hand) slept in the hall, since the thieves had taken Mirita's home and car keys. The next day, I called a locksmith and had all the house and car keys changed. The thieves tried to use a card at a gas station, but they failed because I had already canceled them.

Except for this minor incident, we have not had any problems during our lives in the United States. Thank God, we have enjoyed the most precious thing a man cherishes: a family and the possibility to choose and decide what to do with our lives in freedom and democracy.

My daughter Maitelis earned a legal assistant degree. She held her wedding in a very old Coconut Grove house, the backyard of which faces Miami Bay with a unique view. The gorgeous ceremony was held in the backyard conducted by a priest. Several years later she had a very cute, clever, and intelligent son.

My son Hector Eduardo (Eddy), who had taken karate classes as a kid while in Cuba, continued to practice karate for a few years in Miami. Later on, he quit but kept playing other sports. He has won trophies and medals in several local competitions and little leagues in football, softball, and track and field. He also competed in a triathlon, where he had to swim, run, clear hurdles, and ride a bicycle for several miles. Besides, he does weightlift at home, plays golf, practices target shooting, bowling, hunting, fishing, and goes jogging frequently to stay in shape. He's a true athlete.

Eddy majored in accounting and earned a minor in International Relations, and also got a state certificate as CPA. He was offered a position in the Department of Defense Office of Inspector General (DoD OIG), but after thinking about the opportunity and visiting Virginia and Washington, D.C. he decided to remain in Miami near his family and friends, which we praised with joy.

A few years later, he became an accounting partner director in a major international company. He was also the chairman of the Cuban American Certified Public Accountants, ex-chairman of the Miami Downtown Chapter of the Florida Institute's Certified Public Accountants, and one of the directors of the Latin Builders Association. He got married in church and already has four lovely and intelligent children.

All in all, we have five beautiful grandchildren in a free society, which we are very proud of every day, we are grateful to God and more than glad to have had the courage to abandon and escape the Castros' communist dictatorship, and thus give our children the choice to have a better education and future in a democracy in the free land of America.

I worked so hard, about twelve hours a day, that once in a furniture store, while sitting and waiting for customers to come in, I fell half asleep when a friend, Katia Armas, dropped by. Katy, as we call her, approached me to tell me something, which made me jump scared, throwing blows in the air as an unconditioned reflex until I was fully awake and realized it was her. I deeply apologized even though I never hit her. Every time we met; we would laugh while she mimicked boxing moves. She is a kind person, and we love her very much. I occasionally reacted like that as a defense

237

reflex, and for that reason, there were several times when I was close to hitting someone.

Regarding the other two classmates in the International Relations Higher Institute, who were also students from the Marianao High School, I was told, but not confirmed, that Nestor Sosa, after serving in the Cuban embassy in Moscow, reaching the rank of Counselor, either resigned or was expelled from the Foreign Ministry and allegedly lives in the United States. I have never had any contact with him. As to the other one, Rodolfo Blain, who had diplomatic positions in Canada and Lebanon, had died of natural causes.

There is a big number of children and grandchildren of the so-called leaders of the revolution, and generals and other high-profile officials, who have opposed their parents and are now living in the United States and Europe.

The alleged creation of the new man was a total failure for communist leaders, since many young people who are already adults, ended up turning their backs against them.

There are several classmates from my graduation in December 1974 and subsequently others in the International Relations' Higher Institute who became ambassadors, while others have defected or passed away.

Some high-ranked figures of the Cuban regime have had mysterious heart attacks or other health issues. Many Cuban officials who are not members of the repressive apparatus live alienated from the inner problems faced by the Cuban people, closing their eyes to atrocities and abuses. That is why, out of experience, they have inevitably become accomplices. Others enjoy their privilege until the day the diabolic system does away with them, like Saturn devoured his sons in Roman mythology. It is well known that many high-ranking leaders and officials in the Cuban regime were executed by firing squad, disappeared, or suffered from "Health Issues". However, others have gotten illicitly rich and reached such a high standard of living, like that of a successful capitalist businessman, because they corruptly took advantage of their power and high posts. These corrupt individuals are the ones who shore up the Castros' system and some of these are compromised for having blood in their hands. They are responsible for having divided families in the Cuban nation.

Nowadays, due to advanced technology, no matter how hard the Cuban government tries to restrain it, there is some access to the internet and cell phones used by brave dissidents. This is extremely important because as the saying goes "a picture is worth a thousand words".

The world is getting more and more aware of human rights violations in Cuba, such as the government repressive mobs against the peaceful demonstrations of harmless women called "Ladies in White" (a group of women trying to have their relatives, who are political prisoners, released). Also, there has been a way to disseminate more news on the death of political prisoners, and dissidents on hunger strikes due to the lack of the medical attention and abuses committed by the dictatorship.

A team of lawyers in Miami has been collecting, thanks to a state-of-the-art technology, images of repression in Cuba in order to identify the faces of abusive thugs who have carried out beatings and abuses so that one day they can stand trial and pay for their crimes.

Soon, Cuba will be a free democratic and independent country so that families can reunite and get rid of that nightmare which has made a country that was once one of the most prosperous in Latin America, turn backwards for so many years.

According to information and analyses released by economic experts like Jesus Marzo Fernandez, an ex-official of the Cuban government and former representative of Cuba in the then Council of Mutual Economic Assistance of the socialist bloc (Comecon), when the revolution took power in 1959, Cuba was eighty percent food self-sufficient and imported just twenty percent of their consumer needs, mainly goods from Spain. Nowadays, the figures have turned to the opposite, where Cuba imports eighty percent of foodstuffs allotted to the population in limited quantities through the infamous ration card.

While Cuba was in 1959, one of the biggest consumers in Latin America, together with Argentina and Uruguay, today it is at the level of Haiti.

Cuba is practically in a starving stage and industries lack spare parts. Out of the seven million tons of sugar produced in 1959, today hardly a million is produced. There are just a few sugar mills working, while some have been sold to foreign countries, and others have been deactivated over the lack of maintenance.

Due to a ravaged agriculture, a paralyzed industry, a lack of hard currency, purchasing credit, and lack of the people's support for the dictatorship, it is evident that profound changes have to take place in the system, or the Cuban economy might suffer a collapse any time, especially if it lost the daily aid of oil and other staples from their Venezuelan disciples and partners, Nicolas Maduro now and Hugo Chavez before. The Cuban sugar and agriculture ministers have been substituted over twenty times since the revolution took over in Cuba.

Fidel Castro himself directed agricultural plans and took catastrophic and ridiculous measures due to his sick mind. Examples of these are the so-called "Havana Cord", in which all the flora (including fruit trees) surrounding the city was replaced by coffee and pigeon pea plants, among others (a plan that resulted in a flat-out fiasco); dwarf cow crossbreeding to raise them in the backyards; chicken raising and vegetable planting in the yard for self-consumption; and stop sowing sugar cane fields in order to let thick brushwood grow to export it as charcoal, among other things.

In 2008, General Ulises Rosales del Toro was named agriculture minister number 23. General Ulises was the head of the Armed Forces General Headquarters and member of the Communist Party's Politburo.

He was head of the Instruction Special Groups headquarters in Algeria, head of the Troops Group in southern Angola, and carried out a special mission in Venezuela. He was decorated as hero of the Republic of Cuba. However, this general, hero and pride of the Castros brothers, could not solve the agricultural issues. On the contrary, the first quarter of 2010 turned out to be the worst period of any year of the revolution. And as of today, it continues to be the biggest food crisis in the country.

This critical economic and social situation in Cuba is due to the fact that the socialist system definitely does not work and is a total failure.

Every day, when I wake up, I thank God for living in a free country, I ask Him for blessing my family and me, and I pray for the freedom of Cuba.

May God bless America!

Miami, Florida, February 22nd, 2021 (original manuscript in Spanish)

Miami, Florida, June 8th, 2024 *(manuscript modified and translated into English)*

CHAPTER XI

Copies Of Some Photos And Related Press Articles

Photo No. 1

1980. Damascus, Syria. Diplomatic Reception.

Left to right: Holy See Nunciature Counselor; H.E. the Apostolic Nuncio; Author, Mr. Hector G. Aguililla, Cuban Charge D' Affairs a.i Mrs. Miriam Aguililla, Author's wife; and another guest.

Photo No. 2

1980. Damascus, Syria, Diplomatic Reception.

Left to right: Mr. Saleh, Member of the Political Bureau of the DFLP; His Excellency the Hungarian Ambassador; Mr. Nayef Hawatmeh, General Secretary of the DFLP; and the Author, Mr. Hector G. Aguililla, Cuban Charge D' Affairs a.i

Photo No. 3

December 19th, 1983, Damascus, Syria. Diplomatic Reception. Farewell to outgoing Cuban Ambassador by the Dean of the Diplomatic Corps in Syria.

Left to right:

1. Author, Mr. Hector G. Aguililla.
2. Mrs. Miriam Aguililla, Author's wife.
3. Far back left: His Excellency Ambassador of Jordan, Dean of the Diplomatic Corps.
4. His Excellency, outgoing Cuban Ambassador, Mr. Lester Rodriguez Perez.
5. His Excellency, the Chilean Ambassador.

Photo No. 4

*1982, Mezzeh (New Damascus), Syria. The Author,
Mr. Hector G. Aguililla in his Penthouse Residence*

PHOTO No. 5

1986, Tehran, Iran; Diplomatic Reception.

Left to right: Rumanian Minister Counsellor; Author, Mr. Hector G Aguililla, Cuban Charge D'Affairs a.i.; and his wife, Mrs. Miriam Aguililla.

1986, View of the Latyan dam, less than 25 miles from Tehran, Iran.

The Author, Mr. Hector G. Aguililla, and his wife,

Mrs. Miriam Aguililla.

PHOTO No. 7

1987 At the Residence of HE the Ambassador of Venezuela in Tehran, Iran.

Left to right: Author, Mr. Hector G. Aguililla; HE the Ambassador of Venezuela, Mr. Rafael Zanoni; and Mrs. Miriam Aguililla, Author's wife.

Photo No. 8

1988. The Author, Mr. Hector G. Aguililla with his two children, Maitelis (Maite) and Hector Eduardo (Eddy). after arriving from transit made in Frankfurt, Germany, to their first residence in USA (State of Maryland).

Article No.1

The New York Times

January 26, 1989

Cuban Envoy Defects to U.S.

AP

WASHINGTON, Jan. 25— A veteran Cuban diplomat secretly defected to the United States three months ago after becoming disillusioned with widespread official corruption and with Cuban support for Marxist rebels in at least three Latin American countries.

In an interview here, the diplomat, Hector Aguililla Saladrigas, 35 years old, offered details of what he said was Cuba's in cooperation with Palestinian radicals in international arms trafficking.

Mr. Aguililla was granted political asylum by United States officials in October, but his defection was not publicly disclosed until the State Department made him available for the interview Tuesday.

A spokesman at the Cuban diplomatic mission here declined to comment on Mr. Aguililla's assertions.

Mr. Aguililla said that with Palestinian help, Cuba has arranged for the transport of large quantities of Western-made weapon to guerrilla groups in El Salvador, Guatemala and Chile.

He said that from 1980 to 1983, while he served as the second-ranking Cuban diplomat in Damascus, he routinely made trips to the Bekaa in Lebanon, where his car was loaded with rifles, pistols, revolvers and smoke bombs.

Article No. 2

AP

Jan. 26, 1989

Credit...The New York Times Archives

About the Archive

This is a digitized version of an article from The Times's print archive, before the start of online publication in 1996. To preserve these articles as they originally appeared, The Times does not alter, edit or update them.

Occasionally the digitization process introduces transcription errors or other problems; we are continuing to work to improve these archived versions.

A veteran Cuban diplomat secretly defected to the United States three months ago after becoming disillusioned with widespread official corruption and with Cuban support for Marxist rebels in at least three Latin American countries.

In an interview here, the diplomat, Hector Aguililla Saladrigas, 35 years old, offered details of what he said was Cuba's in cooperation with Palestinian radicals in international arms trafficking.

Mr. Aguililla was granted political asylum by United States officials in October, but his defection was not publicly disclosed until the State Department made him available for the interview Tuesday.

A spokesman at the Cuban diplomatic mission here declined to comment on Mr. Aguililla's assertions.

Mr. Aguililla said that with Palestinian help, Cuba has arranged for the transport of large quantities of Western-made weapons to guerrilla groups in El Salvador, Guatemala and Chile.

Off the record - press ignores defected Cuban diplomat Hector Aguililla Saladrigas

National Review, Feb 24, 1989

A FEW MONTHS AGO a veteran Cuban diplomat named Hector Aguililla Saladrigas secretly defected to the United States, bringing with him a good bit of useful intelligence. For instance, as Associated Press reported after an interview with Mr. Aguililla, there is "the role Cuba has played in cooperation with Palestinian radicals in the shadowy international arms-trafficking business." It turns out that from 1980 to 1983, as Cuba's second-ranking diplomat in Syria, Mr. Aguililla participated in a scheme by which Marxist Palestinian groups supplied Cuba with guns and high-powered weaponry for re-export to Chile, El Salvador, and Guatemala. These were chiefly Western-made weapons, he explained, to conceal "socialist involvement" in case of discovery. For its part, Cuba has returned the favor by offering the Palestinians "training of a terrorist nature" and-for slow learners-instruction in such basics as falsifying passports and invisible writing.

This story was printed, at full length or nearly so, in the Miami Herald, the Chicago Tribune, the Houston Chronicle, and the Washington Times, among other big-city newspapers. But the Washington Post, the Boston Globe, and the Los Angeles Times each apparently deemed the piece unfit to print, while the New York Times reserved a shrunken six inches for it in the middle of page ten. One might assume that these "papers of record" elected not to use the story in a lofty disdain for wire copy, intending to get their own reporters on it directly. So far, alas, nothing. Likewise, the networks and panel-discussion programs all had better things to cover.

In the case of the New York Times, the explanation was clear enough. The front page that same day brought yet another "dramatic disclosure" concerning Chilean diplomat Orlando Letelier, whose death 12 years ago is presumed to be a source of continued torment for us all. This twenty-inch rehash of a Chilean government official's admission of complicity in Letelier's death-a story of real but modest interest-was treated as news of the greatest moment.

There is, of course, no liberal bias here, merely liberal news judgment. The Aguililla interview was a genuine news story, about events likely, in the long run, to affect and perhaps end the lives of many truly innocent people throughout Latin America. There were unanswered questions galore. How much lethal weaponry has this Cuban-Palestinian smuggling network already shipped into the region? How and where has it been put to use? How many people have been killed as a result? Is this still going on? To find the answers, readers of our distinguished papers of record must turn elsewhere. Until justice has been done for Letelier, such peripheral matters will just have to wait.

Article No. 4
WORLD & NATION

The World - News from Jan. 27, 1989

L.A. Times Archives

Jan. 27, 1989, 12 AM PT

A Cuban diplomat who defected to the United States said he took part regularly in a Palestinian-backed, Cuban gun-running operation to rebel groups in three Latin American countries. Hector Aguililla Saladrigas, 35, said that with Palestinian help, Havana arranged to ship large quantities of Western-made weaponry to guerrilla groups in El Salvador, Guatemala and Chile. He also said that Cuba provides "terrorist" training to Palestinian militants. Aguililla, who spent most of his 14-year diplomatic career involved in Middle East affairs, said he defected after becoming disillusioned with his government.

Article No. 5

(See below for an unofficial translation)

UNOFFICIAL TRANSLATION (Article No.5)

TUESDAY, FEBRUARY 7th, 1989

The Soviets Need Peace

Cuban ex-diplomat Hector Gustavo Aguililla Saladrigas defected in October 1988 with his wife and his children on his way to a post in the Cuban Embassy in Madagascar. This interview reports the circumstances which led him to exile and the regime's undercover political activities under which he lived during his thirty-five years.

Q: How are Cuba's relations with the Palestinian Liberation Organization (PLO)?

A: They are good but cautious. We did not see Yasser Arafat as a reliable man. We knew about his homosexual trends because the Palestinians themselves told us, but our fear was of a different kind. We saw the PLO as an opportunistic mixture of several groups and Arafat at as political chameleon who disguised as a communist in Moscow, as a fundamentalist in Saudi Arabia, and acted as a capitalist in Washington. His interest is to be head of state of the capitalist nation without caring too much about the compromises that laid ahead.

Q: Who are the candidates Cuba has in mind in this conflict?

A: Our best relations are with the Popular Front for the Liberation of Palestine (FPLP) led by George Habache and, above all, with the Democratic Front for the Liberation of Palestine (FDLP) of Nayef Hawatmeh. That is our man because he is Moscow's, too. He is a disciplined Marxist.

Q: And Abu Nadel?

A: There are relations with him but very secret ones.

Q: Have you said that Hawatmeh's FDLP is the party Moscow supports? Has its support changed ever since the appearance of the perestroika and the changes that Gorbachev propel?

A: I don't think Moscow will stop supporting the Palestinians' cause because I've already told you our analysis is that it is a conflict that weakens the West, enrages it, and exacerbates contradictions among capitalist countries, but, however, it is true that the USSR is clamoring for peace. I have spoken with my Soviet counterparts about these topics and even the USSR' Foreign Ministry sent high-ranking officials to Cuba to explain Gorbachev's new position. And the reasoning they are expressing is coherent. The Soviets claim they need peace because the imperialist countries' economies are bolstered with the arms race, while the socialist countries' economies dwindle in that respect. That's why the revolutionary thinking right now is to reach an understanding with the West and temporarily stop the military competition and cold war to be able to reinvigorate the economies of communist countries.

Q" And does Cuba take part in that analysis?

A" No, Castro sees things differently. To Castro, conspiracies and underground activities are the object of his life. Castro has done incredible things regarding that. In 1962, Ambassador Lester Rodriguez told me that, during the missile crisis, Castro sent twins Tony and Patricio LaGuardia to New York with several portfolios full of explosives aimed at blowing the UN building up with all diplomats inside if the United States invaded the island. His theory was that dragging other countries to the conflict, Cuba could save itself. Besides, it there was to be a catastrophe, it would reach everybody.

Q: But doesn't the USSR impose its foreign policy to Cuba?

A: It has influence but it does not impose is foreign policy. Everywhere, the diplomatic corps of socialist countries meet periodically under the tacit leadership of the Soviet delegates who underscore the general schemes of discussions and directives, but these are not mandatory.

Q: Aren't there, then, fissures between the Soviet and Cuban diplomacies?

A: No, not yet.

Q: And South Yemen?

A: South Yemen could become the Cuba of the Arab world. An export model. Yemen even has dittoed the Cuban repressive structure. There you'll find mass organizations like the Defense Committees in each street block, and militias identical to those in Cuba. But tall has ended in economic disaster and a horrible struggle for power. In the '86 civil war, terrible things happened. President Ali Nasser Muhammad gave his bodyguards orders to murder the Politburo members opposing him. There were terrible killings. He himself had to go on exile. The current strongman, Al Beihd, is very pro-Cuban. Many Yemenites have gone to study in Cuba. Castro's links with the communists on that side of the world are very strong. You can't forget that there were Cubans fighting in the Oman Sultanate when the guerrilla fighters in the seventies tried to overthrow Sultan Qabus.

Q: And what was Cuba's participation in the war between Iran and Iraq?

A: Cuba was officially neutral but, in reality, we were closer to Iraq. President Hussein had undergone surgery of a disc hernia by Cuban surgeon Alvarez Cambra.

However, that conflict helped us foster military cadres and physician experts on the effects of conventional warfare of great proportions. In Iran, Cuban doctors studied how to fight those effects and Iraq how to create them.

Q: Does Cuba have chemical weapons?

A: As far as I know, the country is ready to produce them whenever they wish.

Q: What will the effect on your defection be on the Foreign Ministry?

A: Nothing out of the ordinary. After me, others have defected. I guess Barreiro will have to make another video stressing that one can be trusted. And it's true. Otherwise, it would be so easy, one would be tempted to write that after this Aguililla, many will fly. There's no doubt about it.

Article No. 6

(See below for an unofficial translation)

SABADO 4 DE FEBRERO DE 1988
EL NUEVO HERALD **7A**

Castro planeaba volar NU en 62, afirma desertor

Por CARLOS ALBERTO MONTANER
Director de las páginas de Opinión

Washington — Es la crisis de nunca acabar. Ahora acaba de saberse que en octubre de 1962, mientras los delegados ante Naciones Unidas debatían el asunto de los cohetes soviéticos en Cuba, dos altos funcionarios de la inteligencia castrista planeaban la voladura del edificio de NU con todos sus ocupantes dentro.

La revelación ha sido hecha por Héctor Gustavo Aguililla, diplomático cubano de 35 años quien desertó a Estados Unidos en octubre de 1988 acompañado por su mujer y dos hijas.

Según Aguililla, la operación hubiera sido llevada a cabo por los gemelos Tony y Patricio Laguardia, hombres clave de la inteligencia cubana, quienes a la sazón viajaron a Nueva York como diplomáticos del séquito del entonces canciller Raúl Roa, ocultando en el equipaje varias maletas llenas de explosivos.

Aguililla tuvo acceso a esta información durante su estadía en Siria como primer secretario de la embajada cubana en Damasco. Léster Rodríguez, entonces embajador en ese país, le relató el incidente y le explicó la lógica de semejante acción terrorista.

Para Castro —de acuerdo con el testimonio de Aguililla— la única posibilidad de supervivencia que Cuba tendría en caso de una invasión norteamericana estaría en relación directa con las proporciones del caos internacional que la isla fuera capaz de desatar. De ahí el proyecto de dinamitar la sede de NU en Nueva York. Un suceso de esta índole hubiera arrastrado al conflicto a numerosas naciones y hubiera impedido un desigual mano a mano entre Cuba y Estados Unidos.

Las revelaciones de Aguililla, por otra parte, parecen confirmar la belicosa actitud exhibida por Castro durante aquellos peligrosos días de octubre de 1962. Recientemente un hijo de Nikita Kruschev declaró —aunque más tarde lo desmentiría— que Castro le había pedido a su padre que lanzara sobre las ciudades norteamericanas los misiles instalados en la isla.

Otro elemento novedoso introducido por Aguililla en el análisis de aquellos acontecimientos tiene que ver con el derribo del avión U-2 ocurrido en medio de la crisis. Según el diplomático cubano, la base desde donde se dispararon los misiles que destruyeron el avión espía norteamericano era operada conjuntamente por soviéticos y cubanos, siendo estos últimos, y por órdenes expresas de Castro, quienes tomaron la iniciativa de atacar la nave norteamericana. Los rusos tenían instrucciones de no hacerlo.

UNOFFICIAL TRANSLATION (Article No. 6)

SATURDAY, FEBRUARY 4TH 1989

EL NUEVO HERALD　　　　　7A

Castro planned to blow the UN up in 1962, defector claims.

By Carlos Alberto Montaner, Director of Opinion pages

Washington. It Is the never-ending crisis. Now, we just found out that in 1962, while the delegates to the United Nations debated the Soviet missiles situation in Cuba, two high-profile officers of Castro's intelligence were planning to blow up the UN building with everyone inside.

The revelation has been made by Hector Gustavo Aguililla, a thirty-five-year-old Cuban diplomat who defected to the United States in October 1988. Accompanied by his wife and two children.

According to Aguililla, the operation would have been carried out by twins Tony and Patricio LaGuardia, key men in Cuban intelligence, who at the time traveled to New York as diplomats in the entourage of then Foreign Minister Raul Roa, hiding in their baggage several bags full of explosives.

Aguililla had access to this information during his stay in Syria as First Secretary in the Cuban Embassy in Damascus. Lester Rodriguez, at that time, Ambassador in that country, told him about the incident and explained this logic behind such terrorist attack.

To Castro, according to Aguililla's testimony, the only possibility of survival in Cuba would have in case of a U.S. aggression, would be directly related to the magnitude of international chaos the island would be able to unleash.

Thus, the project to dynamite the UN headquarters in New York. An event of these proportions would have dragged many nations into the conflict and would have prevented an unequal tete-a-tete between Cuba and the United States.

The revelations by Aguililla, on the other hand, seem to confirm the bellicose attitude by Castro during those dangerous days of October 1962. Recently, a son of Nikita Khruschev declared- although later denied by him- that Castro had asked his father to launch the missiles existing in the island against U.S. cities.

Another novel element presented by Aguililla in the analysis on those events has to do with the shooting down of a U2 plane during the crisis. According to the Cuba diplomat, the base from where the missile shots that destroyed the U.S. spy plane were made, was jointly operated by Soviets and Cubans, with the latter, by expressed orders of Castro, taking the initiative to attack the U.S. aircraft. The Russians had orders to not do it.